WHEN WE LET GO

The Quiet Collapse of Effort, Ambition, and Responsibility

Renae C. Linde

CRF Luttrell

Copyright © 2025 by Cynthia RF Luttrell

ISBN: 979-8-9930830-3-2

All rights reserved.

No portion of this book may be reproduced, stored, or transmitted in any form or by any means, electronic, mechanical, photocopying, recording, or otherwise, without the prior written permission from the copyright owner, except in the case of brief quotations embodied in reviews or articles as permitted by U.S. copyright law.

Independent Publication by CRF Luttrell

contents

Introduction	1
PART I The Withering Will	7
1. The Choice Not to Try	9
2. The Damsel, the Knight, and the Shadow of Dependency	21
3. When Effort Became Optional	31
PART II The Inheritance of Less	39
4. What We Pass Down Without Meaning To	41
5. Children and the Echo of Adult Abdication	55
6. Screens as Surrogates, Silence as Strategy	67
PART III Systems That Keep Us Small	77
7. Disability, Despair, and the Disappearing Line	79
8. The Performance of Powerlessness	91

9. Dreams Without Work	103
PART IV The Road We're Walking	115
10. From Survival to Surrender	117
11. The Lives That Don't Build Anything	129
12. How We Might Begin Again	139
Concluding Thoughts	149
References	157

Introduction

This book began with a pattern I couldn't ignore. One branch of a family tree simply stopped growing. There was no ongoing crisis. It didn't happen overnight, but through small pauses that added up. Effort went first, quietly, almost politely. Responsibility followed, and then initiative. Parents began avoiding conflict. Children began floating through it. Excuses layered one atop another until they hardened into something that felt like truth. The other branches, still flawed, still human, kept moving anyway. They bent, they broke, they mended. But this one didn't. It withered while the others worked. The difference wasn't luck or trauma. It was posture.

I've watched what happens when help turns into habit. A woman in our extended family and her grown son were offered every chance to stabilize: long talks, financial support, even a fully paid mobile home. Each time, they promised to improve. Promised to follow through. And each time, nothing changed.

The car title went untransferred. Rent went unpaid. The son, an adult by every measure, talked about getting a job but never moved. He said he was "waiting." His mother worked just enough to get by, never more.

The weight didn't fall only on them. It landed on everyone who kept trying to help. Over time it became clear this wasn't a rough patch, it was a way of life. A quiet arrangement built from avoidance, dependence, and the unspoken idea that effort was optional as long as someone else stayed responsible.

Another relative made the same pattern impossible to ignore. Given shelter, a car, and a simple agreement, stay here, find work, save, move forward, she did none of it. Months passed. No plan. No motion. When asked to honor the deal or move out, she erupted. Not in sadness, but in rage. Words flew. Violence followed.

That was the turning point. The offer of help hadn't been received as opportunity. It had been taken as obligation, ours, to absorb whatever they refused to face. Effort wasn't missing. It was rejected. The more we stepped back, the faster they unraveled. But every push toward responsibility was treated as betrayal.

For years, I heard stories like this from a distance. Headlines. Conversations. Parents sighing about adult children who wouldn't launch, or children whispering about parents who wouldn't lead. I listened, nodded, and quietly felt lucky. That wasn't us. My upbringing hadn't bred helplessness. My children had grown. The pattern, I thought, belonged elsewhere.

That comfort lasted until it didn't. The same drift appeared close to home, soft dependencies, fading urgency, a sense that effort had become optional. It didn't crash in. It seeped in. And that familiarity was the warning.

The image that came to me was this: a rotting branch on a living tree. A family, like a tree, reaches in many directions. Some limbs strengthen, others split, most bend. But when one stops reaching and starts to decay, the damage doesn't stay contained. Left alone, rot spreads inward. It weakens the trunk. It drains what's still alive. The dying branch doesn't just fail, it feeds on the rest.

This book follows the slow cost of that burden: how it spreads, who it changes, and what it leaves behind.

Not long ago, this wasn't how people thought. After the Depression and the war, hardship had weight, a kind of presence you could feel. Everyone when through it; it was training. Survival meant showing up, contributing, pulling your share of the load. Children learned early what needed to be done and did it. Young adults married, worked, built homes not because it was romantic, but because it was required. The ethic of that time was rough around the edges, sometimes even cruel, but it was clear enough: grow up, help out, keep moving. Independence wasn't a goal. It was assumed.

By 2020, more than half of Americans between eighteen and twenty-nine had moved back under their parents' roofs. This is the highest number recorded since the Great Depression (Fry, 2020). Money explains part of it, but what's changed is the shape of adulthood itself. It used to be a crossing defined by taking on work, responsibility, and risk. What felt like a rite passage has become a slow drift. Responsibility, now feels optional or indefinitely postponed. For many, it never quite arrives. The obstacles aren't only economic; they're internal, the quiet absence of preparation for what to do once the safety net becomes home again. They were never trained to move through them.

A 2023 study found that over forty percent of Americans under thirty-five report "chronic emotional dependency" on parents or partners (Taylor & Blum, 2023). This is disintegration, self-regulation replaced by crisis, crisis answered by caretakers. Dependency, once shameful, is now met with sympathy. Over time, it wins permission. These aren't people faking helplessness. They've simply never been expected to stop being helped.

This book doesn't hand out steps or strategies. It isn't a guide for parents or a pep talk for the unmotivated. It won't paint the past as golden or the present as doomed. What it does is trace a posture, a cultural lean, not toward catastrophe, but away from growth.

What's eroding isn't productivity. It's identity. When trying becomes rare, trying becomes radical. When children grow up uncorrected, resilience doesn't lag behind, it vanishes. And when systems soothe dysfunction instead of confronting it, dependence hardens into lifestyle, and dysfunction becomes inheritance.

Each chapter moves outward, from the personal to the systemic to the speculative. We begin with the quiet disappearance of effort, then follow how helplessness becomes habit: first in families, then in institutions that adjusted downward instead of holding their line.

Later, we'll look at the emotional toll. What becomes of a child raised by silence? What fills the space when structure disappears?

How do screens and social scripts reshape attention, discipline, and the ability to connect?

Finally, we'll look forward. If one rotting branch can drain a tree, what happens when whole limbs begin to fail? What happens when dysfunction's weight rests on those still carrying? When surrender starts to masquerade as wisdom?

This book isn't about blame. It's about consequence. It's for those who have watched this drift in classrooms, families, churches, workplaces, for those who still believe effort matters, and who sense that culture changes not through revolutions, but through routines. It's for the tired carriers who wonder if anyone else sees the weight.

The question is no longer, *What went wrong?*

The question is, *What happens when we stop expecting anything at all?*

PART I THE WITHERING WILL

THE CHOICE NOT TO TRY

When Effort Slipped Away

Once, effort was simply the weather of life, steady, unremarkable, expected. You rose, dressed, and carried the weight in front of you. Trying wasn't a declaration of character; it was the quiet rhythm that kept a day upright. People didn't look for meaning in the work. The work was meaning enough. There were no manuals for persistence, no language for refusal. You did what needed doing because that's what kept the world turning.

Ambition used to carry a certain dignity. It meant wanting to grow, to build, to reach beyond the border of what you already knew. Now it's often treated like a kind of contagion, too sharp, too individual, too invasive to the emotional balance people are trained to protect.

Over the past decade, drive has become suspect. Not banned, success is still allowed, but the way you reach it has changed. You can stumble into it. Manifest it. Be lifted by luck or algorithm. But if you grind for it, if you plan, sweat, and sacrifice, people look at you sideways. They wonder what's wrong underneath. What are you escaping? Who did you step over? What pain are you trying to prove away?

I knew a young man once, let's call him Connor. He'd always had a quiet fire in him. He took honor classes, had a part-time job, and even volunteered on weekends. His parents didn't push him; he pushed himself. In high school, that kind of drive drew respect. But college was different. His new circle was filled with bright, sensitive individuals. Fluent in all the right cultural cues, who talked often about rest, balance, the need to resist "the grind." At first, Connor just listened. Then he started quoting the same phrases. He missed deadlines. He talked about burnout and systems and the moral importance of slowing down. Eventually, he left school, not in defeat, but in declaration. He hadn't failed, he said. He had opted out.

Now, he lives at home. He's settled. He picks up small projects here and there, and helps out around the house when asked. He's online, active, and informed, but the line of his life now runs flat. The change in him isn't viewed as loss, it's praised. "At least he's not stressed," people say. "At least he's not stuck in some corporate grind." Connor didn't lose ambition. He learned that having it made people uneasy.

There's no villain here. No collapse. Just a shift in what effort means. In many circles, exertion now signals imbalance. If you're always pushing, you must be compensating. If you keep striving, maybe something's wrong with you. Effort used to reveal direction; now it's interpreted as unrest.

What's sold as a softer way of living is, in truth, an agreement to move together at the same gentle pace. Ambition disrupts that rhythm. It makes others restless. The one who pushes too hard breaks the illusion that everyone's fine as they are. To keep things even, effort must be disguised.

You can still succeed, but not too visibly. You can grow, as long as it looks effortless. You can rise, but you'd better have a soft story to go with it, trauma, burnout, self-reinvention, something that rounds off the edge. Raw ambition sounds abrasive now, almost accusatory, as if the simple act of striving were an insult to the unhurried.

That's the change. Effort used to speak for itself. Now it needs softening, an explanation, almost an apology. Not to employers or systems, but to the people watching. The sight of steady work makes them uneasy. The very posture that once held families together, that built trades and towns, now lands wrong in the room. The ones who still show up tired, who keep their word, who build through the ache, there's something about them that unsettles others. Their steadiness feels like accusation. Their discipline, a quiet kind of betrayal. Their pace, out of step with the age.

This isn't rebellion. It's the quiet exit from effort. No protest, no noise, just a slow recalibration of what earns respect until striving feels intrusive.

The culture that once praised perseverance now frames it as pathology. Work hard enough and someone will ask if you're overcompensating. Want more and they'll wonder who you're trying to impress. The low bar, once a sign of failure, now feels like safety. Shared inertia builds camaraderie. When everyone moves slowly, no one has to feel left behind.

Within that shared stillness, complaint becomes community. People bond over how tired they are, how busy, how unfair the system feels. Effort becomes the outlier. When someone breaks the rhythm, stays late, studies more, wants better, the group doesn't say, teach me how you do it. They say, who do you think you are?

The pressure doesn't fall from above; it comes from the circle we want to stay inside. Belonging asks for compromise, not courage. We learn to dim the spark a little, to hide our drive so no one has to feel lesser in its light. To stay likable, effort has to sound accidental, brushed off with a joke. We praise the outcome and pretend not to see the sweat that made it possible. And so, a generation learns to pretend ease where there is labor, to mask work in casual language, to achieve without appearing ambitious.

But beneath the surface, something vital goes missing. When effort is treated as vanity, discipline withers into self-consciousness. People stop trying in plain view. They move quietly, privately, so they won't offend the atmosphere of ease. And slowly, the culture forgets what steady striving looks like, how it shapes character, how it feeds meaning.

The result isn't peace. It's sameness. Ambition unsettles the room; restraint keeps it calm. Trying too hard is no longer a virtue, it's a social breach. The unspoken rule is simple: move, but not faster than the herd.

Most people aren't ashamed of that. They defend it. The low standard feels kind. It demands nothing, forgives everything, and keeps everyone comfortable. But comfort has a cost. It breeds fragility where endurance once lived. The longer we stay at rest, the heavier motion feels.

There was a time when trying wasn't treated as a statement. You worked because the work mattered. You showed up because showing up was the hinge that kept life turning. Somewhere along the way, we began treating that hinge as ornamental. We replaced it with talk of balance and energy, as though preservation were progress.

I think about Connor from time to time. Not as a failure, but as a signpost. His life isn't tragic. It's tidy, calm, manageable. Yet the current that once pulled him forward has stilled, and those who love him have accepted it as wisdom. He is not adrift, but neither is he growing.

That, to me, is the quiet truth hiding inside this cultural moment: we have learned to praise the absence of strain. We've mistaken rest for peace, disengagement for insight, withdrawal for self-awareness. The pursuit of ease has replaced the pursuit of purpose.

When effort slips away, it doesn't make a sound. It leaves behind a gentler rhythm, a lighter load, a calmer room. But under that calm, the structure weakens. A world that no longer expects effort doesn't collapse all at once. It softens, until motion itself feels out of place.

And that is how decline begins, not with rebellion, not with failure, but with agreement. A collective exhale that goes on too long. A generation that confuses stillness for safety, and forgets that every form of growth, every repair, every survival, starts with the same simple act: someone deciding to try again.

The Language of Stepping Back

The slide away from effort didn't arrive through exhaustion alone. It came through words, gentle, reasoned, self-assured words that gave retreat a moral shape. Somewhere along the way, a shared language emerged that made withdrawal sound enlightened. What once described healing now describes avoidance. The vocabulary of recovery became a creed, not of repair, but of retreat.

"Overwhelm." "Regulation." "Triggered." "Toxic." "Unsafe."

Once, these words belonged to the rooms where real wounds were named. They were never meant for convenience; they were a kind of scaffolding, language built to steady people in crisis. But over time, the words drifted out into casual use and changed direction. They stopped describing pain and started excusing distance.

You hear it everywhere now. Someone says they're "protecting their peace" by slipping away without a word. A small disagreement is called "unsafe." What used to be boundaries, simple lines meant to keep relationships clean, have grown into walls against everyday friction. The words still sound calm, even kind, but they don't mean what they used to. They're less about honesty now, and more about escape. They no longer describe emotion; they defend avoidance. They turn discomfort into evidence that you were right to step away.

Therapeutic language carries weight. It sounds official, immovable. It borrows the authority of psychology without needing to earn it. That's why it spreads so easily, it offers cover. You can decline, deflect, detach, and still sound thoughtful. You can opt out of effort without admitting you're afraid to try. It lets you sound compassionate while avoiding contact.

But what we're living through isn't just the rise of a few overused words. It's a larger linguistic shift. As emotional safety becomes our highest good, ordinary friction starts to feel pathological. Disagreement is reclassified as damage. Tension as trauma. Work as wound. In that logic, the only virtuous move left is retreat.

The irony runs deep: the same words that once guided people back toward life are now used to justify leaving it.

It makes me think of Jeanine, a woman I once knew who liked to call herself "chronically overwhelmed." She could hold a room when she wanted to, quick mind, clear voice, steady in conversation. But the moment a deadline came near, something in her collapsed. She'd go quiet as if the simple weight of being counted on was more than she could hold. "I just can't deal with this right now," she'd say, smiling faintly, as though it were self-awareness instead of avoidance.

In time, the phrase stopped needing context. It wasn't a cry for help; it was an ending. Her friends stopped asking. Coworkers stopped expecting. Even she stopped questioning it. "Overwhelmed" had become her identity, her reason not to move.

That's the quiet danger of therapy-speak once it leaves its proper home. It arrests motion. It lets people pause indefinitely, without ever calling it avoidance. The words sound wise, even kind, but they replace the work of recovery with the performance of reflection.

There's a cost for that convenience. When every reaction is treated as diagnostic, growth slows to a crawl. "I don't have capacity" becomes a boundary line that never shifts. "I'm triggered" becomes a full stop instead of an opening. These sentences end the conversation that effort was meant to continue.

This isn't cynicism toward real pain. Nor is it judgment of those who use such language sincerely. It's a caution about what happens when the vocabulary of trauma becomes a trend, when it circulates unexamined, repeated until it loses its gravity and gains authority it was never meant to have.

We're living through that inversion now. Words meant to steady people through crisis are being used to rationalize fragility as permanence. That doesn't protect anyone. It confines them. When discomfort becomes identity, adaptation stops. When avoidance is moralized, resilience withers quietly in the corner.

So we build smaller lives. We narrow our worlds. We decline invitations that might stretch us. We call this peace. We call it alignment. It sounds mature, but it's really a soft surrender. And under the language of self-preservation, something vital goes missing, the impulse to face the edge and grow. The words that once helped people find their footing now hold them still, polishing the glass wall between survival and living.

When Stepping Back Became a Virtue

Somewhere along the cultural line, non-effort crossed a strange threshold. It stopped being neutral and started sounding noble. Pulling away, once a quiet personal decision, now carries moral weight. The person who withdraws, who says no, who bows out of difficulty, is described as wise. Stillness has become a symbol of enlightenment. We speak of detachment with a kind of reverence, as if retreat itself were a higher form of living rather than a strategy for avoiding strain.

This inversion didn't arrive overnight. It was taught back to us, one reinforcement at a time, socially, digitally, institutionally. The one who keeps showing up, who presses for change or refuses to coast, is often seen as rigid. Unyielding. Out of sync with the softer rhythm of things. But the one who steps aside, who drops the weight, who claims to have "done enough," is celebrated as someone who finally understands.

There's truth in the idea that we all need to let go sometimes. But we've gone further, we've turned surrender into superiority.

Listen to how we talk about the ones who stop trying. They've had enough. They're protecting their peace. They're doing what's best for them. No one asks what that choice costs, or who quietly fills the gaps they leave behind. The pause sounds healthy until you're the one picking up what they put down.

In this new moral order, withdrawal reads as virtue. You earn credit not for showing up, but for refusing. You're not difficult. You're not demanding. You don't disrupt the room. You've learned to "honor your limits." The language is soft, but the message is clear: know your place, and don't make others uncomfortable by reaching beyond it.

No one calls it quitting anymore. They call it wisdom. They say you've finally got your priorities straight. But what it really protects isn't peace, it's comfort. Theirs, and yours.

Avoidance doesn't look like much when everyone practices it. It looks like calm. It sounds like balance. But silence, multiplied, becomes decay. When no one moves, we stop expecting motion at all.

I think of a man I once knew. Late forties. Divorced. Kind. Capable. Once owned a small business. Worked with his hands, taught kids in the neighborhood how to fix things. He wasn't loud or boastful, just steady. Then something shifted. He started taking long walks instead of jobs. Talked often about being burned out, about how broken the system was. He said he was protecting his energy.

His friends admired him for it. "He's finally grounded," they said. His ex-wife saw it differently. "He didn't leave," she told me.

"He just let life move on without him." He wasn't cruel. He just stopped being useful.

He'd built a life around avoiding pressure. Responsibility felt like confinement. Expectation, like threat. He wasn't lazy, he was careful. Too careful. He did less and called it peace. And from a distance, it looked serene. But up close, the spark was gone.

That kind of stillness doesn't just happen. It's learned. Reinforced by a culture that applauds the absence of effort as a sign of maturity. We've turned fatigue into philosophy. What once marked rest between seasons of labor has become a permanent state of retreat.

What's missing in all this praise for letting go is an honest look at who's left to carry the load. When someone steps back and calls it balance, someone else quietly steps forward to keep things running. Partners absorb more. Workplaces soften standards. Systems bend. Each accommodation, made in compassion, lowers the collective threshold for effort.

Soon, expectation itself starts to feel aggressive. Trying becomes the odd behavior in the room. Ambition, a kind of indecency. The few who keep pushing learn to do it quietly, so they don't disturb the climate of rest.

And that is how culture drifts, not through crisis, but through comfort. In repetition. A little less drive here. A little more praise for stepping back there. The current changes, degree by degree, until the direction that once pulled us forward feels unnatural to swim toward.

We forget what it's like to want something enough to work for it without irony or apology. We forget that movement itself was once the moral act, the proof that we were still alive to the work of becoming.

THE DAMSEL, THE KNIGHT, AND THE SHADOW OF DEPENDENCY

The Loop of Rescue and Resentment

Some people never had to learn how to try. Trying, for them, wasn't part of the bargain. Struggle showed up, and someone else took the reins. Deadlines were extended. Mistakes were cleaned up. Emotional fallout was managed in the background. Progress was praised even when it wasn't earned. Eventually, effort became optional, and then unfamiliar.

What began as responsiveness became arrangement. The white knight didn't arrive all at once, he stepped in gradually, one quiet intervention at a time. The damsel didn't set out to be rescued. But when the world kept meeting her weakness with warmth, it made sense to stay there. Why fight dragons when someone else handles them better?

In homes like this, helplessness doesn't sound alarms. It's normalized. One person struggles, and the others adjust. The missed appointments, the unkept jobs, the constant volatility, these become weather patterns. Everyone learns to carry an umbrella.

At first, the rescues feel like care. Needs are met. Emotions are tended. Stability holds. But over time, the damsel's world shrinks. She forgets how to carry her own weight. The longer others keep stepping in, the less equipped she becomes to step up.

Dependence becomes identity. Not always declared, but deeply held. And it's easy to justify, especially when it works. When people keep showing up. When the consequences never arrive. When emotional retreat earns comfort, indulgence, and endless patience.

After a while, she doesn't prepare for outcomes, she prepares for rescue. If the knight is slow to appear, she escalates. Anxiety sharpens. Sadness deepens. Rage surfaces. Whatever summons help.

She may not see it that way. She may feel genuinely overwhelmed. But pattern does not wait for intention. It repeats what has worked.

The knight, for his part, doesn't see it as rescue, not right away. He tells himself he is her provider, her protector. He's doing the right thing. She needs him and showing love means shielding her from hardship. But every rescue leaves a scar he can't see. What once felt gallant begins to feel like duty. And the woman he once lifted from the wreck starts to feel less like a companion and more like a weight he can't put down.

Still, he keeps doing it. Each effort heavier, slower. Walking away doesn't feel kind. It feels cruel. The longer he's carried her, the less he remembers what it was like to let his own arms rest. Resentment doesn't roar; it settles, grain by grain. Most men in his place don't make speeches or slam doors. They just grow quiet. Their eyes lose their reach. What remains is a man worn thin by someone else's unfinished growing.

When he finally pulls back, the damsel doesn't interpret it as a call to rise. She interprets it as betrayal. The withdrawal of help feels like abandonment. Her survival has been outsourced for so long that being asked to manage herself registers as cruelty.

Accusations surface. "You don't care." "You left me." "You think you're better than me." She may not mean to manipulate. She may not even hear herself. She simply doesn't know how to function without being rescued.

And now, for the first time, neither does he.

It looked like love from the outside. Safety isn't what was preserved, it was limitation. The connection didn't deepen. It circled. Over time, they stopped becoming more whole and started becoming more useful to the pattern that kept them stuck.

Bowen observed that in families and relationships, one person's constant compensation often enables another's passivity (Bowen, 1978). The system seeks stability, not development. As long as someone is over-correcting, the imbalance can continue quietly, indefinitely.

But stability isn't health. It's delay. And when the rescuer stops rescuing, the system convulses.

Someone eventually steps out of the loop. Sometimes it's the knight. Sometimes it's the damsel, though that's less common. When it happens, the arrangement begins to fail. The rescues dry up. The dependency is exposed. And both are left to face what the rescues were hiding all along: not incapacity, but inertia. Not helplessness, but the habit of being helped. And behind that habit is a system that quietly rewards whoever stays small enough to be carried.

Helplessness by Gender

Not all dependency looks the same. Some of it cries. Some of it vanishes.

In most households shaped by traditional roles, female helplessness is emotional. Visible. Even validated. A girl who cries is comforted. A woman who folds under pressure is excused. She's "sensitive." "Just needs support." "Going through a lot." Her helplessness becomes a call to gather. To soften. To protect.

In that same household, a boy who shows weakness is told to "man up." If he cries, he's sent outside. If he struggles, it's assumed he'll figure it out. Emotional helplessness is not encouraged in boys, but circumstantial helplessness is. They're excused from tasks. "He's just not good at that stuff." "That's not really his thing." "He was never taught." Instead of learning how to stay present in discomfort, they learn how to be buffered from it.

By the time they become adults, the contrast has calcified. Women over-apologize for having needs. Men under-recognize that they have them. The emotional labor is not just unbalanced, it's gendered.

In partnership, this often plays out in familiar ways. She senses the conflict before he does. She brings it up. He shuts down. She becomes the manager of repair. He waits until the air clears. Eventually, she handles it all. He didn't ask her to, but he didn't step in.

And so the loop continues. Her over-functioning becomes the reason he never has to change.

There's a certain kind of man who forgets his child's doctor appointment, can't name the school principal, and refers to parenting as "helping out." He doesn't raise his voice. He's not hostile. He's "easygoing." But every gap he leaves is filled by someone else. Usually, a woman.

There's also a certain kind of woman who texts her adult brother to remind him of their mother's birthday, books the family vacations, calls the pharmacy, remembers the hard dates for everyone but herself. She is not thanked. She is depended on. Quietly. Constantly. Without pause.

In both cases, helplessness becomes part of the system. Not declared. Inferred. The woman who disappears in tears is given space. The man who disappears in silence is given the benefit of the doubt. One becomes responsible for everyone's temperature. The other gets to ignore the thermostat.

It's not always male-female. But the pattern repeats enough to matter. Women are more likely to be trained into regulation. Men are more likely to be excused from it.

What makes this dynamic so durable is that it doesn't present as dysfunction. It presents as compatibility. One person seems good at handling things. The other "isn't wired that way." No one questions it. Not until the one who's handling everything starts to fray.

Underneath it all is a cultural narrative: some people are just more equipped. But that's a lie built on exposure. Resilience isn't innate. It's practiced. The person who holds more does so because they've had to.

Carol Gilligan wrote that women often define themselves through relationship, while men define themselves through separation (Gilligan, 1982). That separation includes the ability to withdraw, without cost. A woman who withdraws is called cold. A man who disengages is "just giving it time."

The cost is subtle, but cumulative. Rescuers lose their sense of fairness. The helpless lose their capacity for growth. What remains is a tired kind of intimacy. Familiar. Asymmetrical. Fragile.

Systems That Bend

Some families don't confront dysfunction. They adjust to it.

Over time, that adjustment becomes structure. Everyone rearranges themselves around the least willing person. Not the most vulnerable, the most immovable. The one who refuses discomfort becomes the one who sets the terms.

I knew a family like this. Three generations shaped by one central pattern: responsibility pooled around avoidance.

The grandmother managed everything. Appointments, money, meals, moods. Her husband smiled through holidays, but rarely lifted a hand. When he grew quiet, she filled the space. When he grew angry, she absorbed it. Her identity became the shape of his absence.

Their daughter vowed not to repeat it. She studied hard. Took initiative. Got out. But the patterns found her anyway. Her husband came with charm, but little follow-through. She made the money. He made excuses. She became "the rock." He became "misunderstood."

She thought her strength would protect her kids from the same story. Instead, it made her indispensable. Her son watched her hold everything and learned that someone always would. Her daughter learned how to pick up what others dropped.

By the time the next generation reached adulthood, the imbalance wasn't new, it was culture. The son couldn't hold a job. Couldn't stay in school. Couldn't regulate his own urgency. But he never lacked support. When he disappeared for a weekend, everyone else shifted plans. When he lashed out, the tension was blamed on stress. When he asked for money, he was helped. Again.

Meanwhile, his sister booked their mother's medical appointments, coordinated holidays, and cleaned up after his emotional damage. Not once did anyone ask if she was okay. She didn't expect them to.

They called her responsible. They called him sensitive. No one called it unfair.

This is how dysfunction survives. Not through chaos, but accommodation. The family system doesn't collapse. It compensates. One person breaks the rhythm, and everyone else learns to dance around it.

Bowen called this the preservation of homeostasis. The system resists change to maintain emotional equilibrium (Bowen, 1978). But equilibrium isn't the same as health. When imbalance is stabilized, dysfunction is prolonged. No one is forced to grow. They're just managed.

In this family, help became harm because no one noticed the cost. The daughter began missing work to manage household crises. The mother stopped going to her own doctor appointments. Everyone carried what he dropped, but no one asked whether he ever planned to pick anything up.

Eventually, the daughter moved away. Quietly. No fight. Just distance.

And in that distance, things unraveled. The mother couldn't keep up. The son grew resentful. He called his sister selfish. Said she had abandoned them. Said she'd "changed."

She had.

What held this system together was silent agreement. That strength was a duty. That weakness was a pass. That fairness was optional. That love meant adaptation.

When one person stopped adapting, the system couldn't hold.

Letting go of the role isn't easy. It feels unnatural at first. Like dropping the rope in a tug-of-war where no one else is pulling. But in time, it's the only move that creates space for change.

Some people will rise when no one rescues them. Some will not. But the possibility only emerges when the pattern is broken. This isn't a story about villains. It's a story about cost. Carried over time. Carried by the same people. And normalized until someone says: No more.

Sometimes, the person who says it isn't thanked. They're resented. They're called disloyal. Cold. Uncaring.

But they are the first person in the system who doesn't bend.

And that's where the strength begins.

WHEN EFFORT BECAME OPTIONAL

The Normalization of Withdrawal

Effort used to be foundational. It wasn't seen as remarkable, just functional. It upheld the daily scaffolding of work, learning, family life. Somewhere along the cultural curve, that foundation cracked. Effort lost its default status and began to look suspicious. In its place, we elevated the language of preservation.

Pulling back used to be a warning sign. Now it's sold as wisdom. People don't say they're tired or avoiding. They don't admit they're checked out. They say they're "protecting their peace," they're "guarding their energy." These aren't coping tools anymore. They've become values. The less you carry, the more grounded you're supposed to be. What used to look like avoidance now gets praised as emotional intelligence.

It didn't start with mental health. It started with lifestyle advice. What was meant to help burned-out people take a step back started showing up everywhere. Articles praised folks for quitting jobs that "didn't serve them" or cutting off anyone who felt "draining." Social media picked it up and ran with it. If something felt hard for too long, the problem wasn't you, it was your surroundings. Sticking it out started to look outdated. Quitting, if you gave it the right name, started to look brave.

There are legitimate reasons to disengage. People should walk away from harmful situations. But we've built an entire language system that frames discomfort as diagnostic. A job that demands too much becomes exploitative. A partner who asks for growth becomes controlling. A friend's neediness becomes toxicity. Withdrawal becomes the signal of health, not harm.

For Sam, a 36-year-old warehouse foreman, this reframe arrived late. He'd built a life around showing up, at work, at home, in crisis. People leaned on him. He didn't complain. He just carried. When burnout hit, he didn't slow down right away. It took two years, a quiet health scare, and some online post about how "always being the one who fixes everything means you're the one who's broken." The way Sam showed up, steady, reliable, used to be respected. Now it was treated like something was wrong with him.

At first, the shift gave him language. Then it gave him an exit. He stopped holding everyone else's weight. He started saying no. But the retreat didn't level him out. It hollowed him. In removing what had once defined his value, he lost more than strain. He lost meaning. "I thought I was doing something to make me more healthy," he told me. "But really, I just stopped being needed."

The culture met him there. Everything in the surrounding discourse reinforced the idea that stepping back was virtuous. There was little inquiry into what might be lost when the steady step away. Sam didn't fall apart, but he did stop building.

Media helped shape the shift. People started saying things like "You don't owe anyone your time," and "If it costs you your peace, it's too expensive." You didn't need a good reason to quit, just the right tone. Nobody asked what happened after. Who stayed. Who adjusted. Fatigue started sounding like wisdom. Staying too long meant you were blind, or worse, being used.

"You shouldn't have to martyr yourself for your job," people said. "Do what you can in the time allowed. The company will still be there even when you're not." What used to sound like burnout management became a philosophy. The subtext was steady: if you're still pushing, maybe you haven't figured it out yet.

Institutions That Adjusted Downward

As the culture softened, institutions followed. But they didn't just respond, they internalized the new avoidance logic. School used to be about getting through it. You were expected to show up, keep up, and deal with whatever was in front of you. More and more, schools are being asked to pay attention to how students feel. Emotional comfort is becoming part of the equation, sometimes even outweighing challenge or performance. It's not that expectations are gone, but they're often softened to avoid pushback or stress.

Grit, or the ability to stick with something hard, is what my grandparents called it. This is what is quietly disappearing. In classrooms, teachers began to re-examine the grading systems that ignored real life: trauma, bad luck, and the uneven starts some kids get. At first, it was about fairness, but then it changed. While assignments stayed long, the urgency to finish them faded. Late work was accepted without much consequence. Teachers were urged through training to weigh not just effort or outcome, but how their tone, their pace, even their expectations might affect a student's peace of mind. The question was no longer, *Can students handle this material?* but *Is this demand fair or harmful given their emotional state or background?*

Angela Duckworth (2016) describes grit not as natural toughness, but as something that can be taught, if it's allowed to be tested. It needs friction. It needs repetition. But in many classrooms, those conditions were removed in the name of emotional safety. The system wasn't just protecting students from failure. It was making strength harder to build.

The same pattern showed up at work. Human resources used to focus on whether people could do the job. Over time, the focus shifted to how people felt while doing it. Emotional safety became part of the conversation. Coaching started to fade. Feedback didn't disappear, but it got vague. Instead of clear direction, you got soft suggestions.

Managers were asked to consider stress, work-life balance, and any outside factors that might explain poor performance. If someone missed the mark, the first response wasn't correction, it was, "Is there anything going on that I should be aware of?" Accountability was still there, but it no longer came first.

When support replaces standards, something slips. People stop knowing where they stand. Expectations blur. Correction gets delayed or skipped. And in time, workplaces that avoid hard conversations don't build stronger teams. They just lower the bar. No one improves, because no one is expected to stretch.

Therapy did not escape the drift. Historically, psychotherapy asked hard questions. It invited discomfort. It guided people through their own contradictions. But the new model, shaped as much by online discourse as clinical tradition, leans increasingly toward affirmation. Sessions circle gently. Therapists validate, soothe, and contain before difficulty fully arrives. Confrontation, once part of healing, now risks sounding unsupportive. Some clients remain in treatment for years without ever being asked to change.

To be clear, therapy should be humane. But it cannot be only that. Without challenge, there is no movement. A therapist who never pushes becomes a witness to decline. An HR department that never draws a line becomes complicit in drift. A school that removes all difficulty stops preparing anyone for the world beyond it.

These institutions did not invent the fragility script. They reinforced it. They built policies that lowered the bar without saying so. What used to count as falling behind got reframed as coping. Over time, easing up became the default. That's how avoidance turned into policy.

The Cost of Making Everything Easier

Language shapes tolerance, but it also shapes suspicion. Once effort became a signal of privilege, expectations themselves came under scrutiny. What once marked commitment, persistence, rigor, delayed gratification, began to look like exclusion. If someone couldn't meet a standard, the fault lay with the standard.

This idea wasn't born in bad faith. Many systems had long privileged speed, conformity, and ease of access to support. Making room for neurodivergence, trauma recovery, and mental health fluctuation was overdue. But in our correction, we adopted a new reflex. What used to be called challenge began to sound like discrimination.

The consequences were subtle at first. A demanding course syllabus triggered student complaints. Teachers who held firm to deadlines faced professional review. Parents who expected chores or self-regulation were told they lacked empathy. Even the work schedule changed. The traditional 9 to 5 gave way to flex time, compressed workweeks, and remote work. While this helped people manage their lives, it also made it harder to name what was expected. When everyone's on a different schedule or in different work environments, accountability gets harder to track. So rather than trying to figure out how to effectively manage such diversities, managers leaned back. The pressure dropped, but so did the structure. Every expectation became suspect. To push was to harm.

This shift wasn't just cultural, it showed up in how people were taught. Haidt and Lukianoff (2018) warned that shielding kids from every kind of discomfort doesn't make them stronger. It makes them afraid of challenge. Instead of learning to handle life, they learn to avoid it.

Inclusion shifted. It stopped being about helping people rise and started being about keeping things easy. Instead of asking how someone could grow into the challenge, we asked whether the challenge should exist at all.

This is the cost. We start to believe that asking someone to struggle is the same as putting them down. That expecting effort is a kind of insult. But growth doesn't happen without tension. And dignity doesn't come from being spared, it comes from facing hard things and knowing you did.

Grit isn't some lost virtue, it's just not expected anymore. In a world where trying too hard makes you look unstable or out of touch, most people stop. We treat pulling back like wisdom and pushing through like a red flag. Systems adjust to whoever struggles the most, then act surprised when no one holds up.

In families, the strongest kid ends up doing the most. In classrooms, the few who can manage on their own get left behind while others get extra help. At work, the ones who keep showing up quietly burn out while everyone else gets praised for "awareness." Eventually, even the steady ones start to wonder what the point is.

It gets called compassion. But really, it's a way of walking away. When we stop believing people can grow, we don't protect them, we erase them. We keep them comfortable, but we keep them small.

We were never meant to live under endless challenge. But we were never meant to live without it.

PART II THE INHERITANCE OF LESS

WHAT WE PASS DOWN WITHOUT MEANING TO

The Curriculum of Behavior

We do not hand failure to our children. We hand them patterns.

What they do with those patterns depends on a thousand quiet factors. Temperament. Timing. Chance. Long before a child forms beliefs, they internalize behaviors. They watch how frustration is handled. They notice who waits. Who wails. Who withholds. They watch what we try for, and what we give up on. They notice whether we keep going after a bad day or shut down the minute things get tough. To a child, effort isn't a concept, it's observable. They're little sponges. They absorb it all, not just what we say, but what we do. What we repeat shapes them.

Most parents don't mean to teach their kids to give up. It just happens slowly. They sidestep hard conversations. Make excuses when things don't work out. Lower the bar instead of holding the line. A child watching this doesn't feel confident. They feel unsure of themselves. The world starts to look bigger than they are. So they copy what they've seen, pulling back, putting things off, falling apart in ways that seem harmless but run deep.

Most parents aren't promoting fragility as a worldview. They're simply enacting it. Over and over. Quietly. Automatically.

A father comes home from work and heads straight to his phone. When his wife asks what's wrong, he waves her off. Says he's tired. The child watches this repeat, day after day, for months. One evening, she's caught breaking a house rule. Her father calls her over. She shrugs, says nothing, then stares at the floor. When he calls her again, firmer this time, she bolts to her room and shuts the door. Later, when asked why she ran, she says she didn't want to make things worse. No tantrum. No explanation. Just learned withdrawal.

What parents frequently label as shyness, or what they call being sensitive, is often something else entirely. It's a child copying what they've seen, pulling back when things get tense, staying quiet to keep the peace.

Children inherit temperament. They develop strategies. Especially those they see reinforced. If an adult handles difficulty by disappearing, the child learns this is how people stay safe. If emotion only shows up when it explodes, the child learns to fear their own build-up. If trying is rarely modeled, they come to believe it doesn't matter.

Much of what we label "fragility" is simply inexperience, children encountering challenge for the first time, with no internal script to meet it.

In this way, love alone doesn't protect a child. Not if that love is fused with patterns that reward retreat. Not if hardship is treated as exceptional instead of inevitable.

The parent who shields their child from all difficulty may believe they are acting from compassion. But over time, this becomes its own quiet curriculum: struggle is danger, feedback is threat, and challenge is personal.

By adolescence, the child will have absorbed this. They may seem articulate. Emotionally literate. They can name their feelings in great detail. But the moment difficulty requires follow-through, they stall. Or spiral. Or shift the blame elsewhere.

This isn't an issue of morality. It's a learned rhythm. They were raised in a system that prioritized calm over formation.

The difference matters. Calm is often momentary. Formation is cumulative. It demands repetition, exposure, and friction. It is not incompatible with warmth, but it does require consistency.

The children who grow up without this tend to sort into one of two groups.

The first becomes performatively incapable. They resist responsibility with a practiced fluency. They describe themselves as overwhelmed by simple tasks. They find relief in being excused, comfort in being coddled. The terms they use to describe their state, words like stressed, scattered, and done, become less about clarity and more about identity. They do not ask how to proceed. They ask to be released.

The second group internalizes a different role. These children become the over-functioners. The quiet siblings. The early achievers. They're often praised for being "so mature" or "easy to raise." What they've learned, in reality, is how to minimize their needs so others don't have to carry them. They scan for stress in the home and compensate for it. As adults, they become exhausted. Polite. Misunderstood.

Both trajectories begin in the same place: a system that trained them to manage stress by themselves.

The parent may not see this. May even resist it. After all, they showed up. They were kind. They used the right words. They never yelled. You can be in the room and still not be emotionally invested. You can love a child deeply and still give them nothing to follow but pushing through or shutting down.

We like to think children absorb our hopes and dreams for them. But they absorb our defaults.

I've seen this play out between two adult sisters in the same extended family, with kids of their own. Rita, the older, stayed consistent and didn't waver. Maggie, the younger, gave in often to keep the peace. Their homes looked similar from the outside. Inside, the tone was entirely different. One taught her children to handle the hard things. The other taught hers to avoid them.

Their contrast matters. One woman wasn't better than the other. But the patterns they practiced shaped everything that followed.

Rita corrected firmly. She followed through. Her children learned that effort was expected even when moods changed. Maggie softened. Explained. Wavered. Her children learned that if you resist long enough, the standard shifts.

The outcomes didn't diverge overnight. They separated slowly, after many tiny pivots. One household, over time, began expecting less. The other, despite setbacks, kept practicing difficulty.

When those children reached adulthood, their realities weren't just different in circumstance. They were different in shape. One was built for resistance. The other, for rescue.

Structure vs. Control

Maggie's story is not unusual. It's just one branch of a pattern seen in thousands of households, where structure is mistaken for being harsh, and discipline as harmful. Her children weren't neglected. They were nurtured gently, but inconsistently. Limits flexed according to the emotion of the moment. Rules were explained but not enforced. Over time, the lessons changed shape.

What started as kindness turned into giving up.

These days, many parents struggle to tell the difference between structure and control. They don't want to be the harsh voice. The one who withholds. They associate firmness with being mean. They equate authority with harm.

So they ask twice, then three, four, five times. They reason. They bribe. They empathize, as if recognition will replace resolve. And when their child resists, they lower or drop the standard altogether to preserve the bond.

They don't mean to teach avoidance, and are probably not even aware that's what they are doing. They just want to stay close.

But saying yes to everything doesn't teach them safety. They learn that from having clear boundaries. They need to know which walls are solid, and which ones collapse under protest.

Marcela, a single mother in her forties, understood this without turning rigid. She worked full-time and raised her two sons in a small apartment above a laundromat. The boys had freedom to explore, to question, to feel, but not to opt out of reality. When they forgot their lunches, she didn't deliver them. When they wanted new shoes before the old ones wore out, she said, "Work with what you have."

One of her sons, angry over a failed test, refused to study for the retake. She didn't argue. She sat at the table and began reading out loud from her own textbook, part of a community college course she took at night. When he asked what she was doing, she said, "I'm studying."

The moment passed. He studied.

Marcela didn't shame her sons. She didn't turn failure into a character flaw. But she didn't stall it either. She made space for their effort to matter. Her children didn't fear her, and they rarely defied her. This wasn't because she was strict, but because she was steady.

The contrast to Maggie wasn't temperament. Both women were warm. The difference was in what each one modeled when things got hard. Maggie leaned in emotionally but bent when it mattered most. Marcela held fast and stayed firm.

This matters more than it first appears. A child raised without structure often grows up believing that defiance is power. If they push hard enough, the world will back down. If they delay long enough, someone else will pick up the slack.

A lot of times, this may look like entitlement. But sometimes it appears as helplessness. A child falls apart when asked to complete a task they've successfully done before. They stall before making decisions. They look for permission to act. It's not that they lack intelligence, but because they were never made to carry forward through pressure.

Parents who worry about being too strict often don't realize what happens when kids grow up without structure. They're trying to make up for the way they were raised, homes that were cold, strict, or full of yelling. So they go the other way. They want their kids to always feel heard. Always feel safe. Always feel okay.

But forming a young mind doesn't always feel good. It stretches. It frustrates. It demands.

That doesn't mean it's cruel. Cruelty aims to break. Formation aims to prepare.

Marcela understood that preparing her sons meant disappointing them sometimes. They weren't entitled to comfort in every moment. They were entitled to clarity.

And clarity is one of the rarest forms of love.

Too many homes today substitute tolerance for clarity. They permit everything to avoid being accused of anything. Over time, the child no longer knows what matters, what lines are fixed, what values are real. Every request becomes a negotiation. Every rule, a mere suggestion.

This erosion happens slowly. A bedtime gets extended once, then always. A consequence gets delayed, then forgotten. A rule is explained again, then ignored. No one calls it backing down. Everyone calls it grace.

But the child registers the shift. They may not celebrate it. They may not trust it. But they learn from it. The lesson is simple: structure is optional.

And if structure is optional, so is personal effort.

Children raised in these environments do not feel more free. They feel more uncertain. They become skilled in manipulating tone, mood, and emotional thresholds, but not in navigating complexity. They become alert to approval, but unaware of endurance.

Eventually, they may even interpret structure as hostility. A teacher who expects more is "mean." A boss who corrects is "unsafe." A partner who holds boundaries is "controlling."

This inversion makes growing up harder. If all pressure feels like punishment, the only thing left that matters is comfort.

What was once a question of discipline becomes a question of identity. The child doesn't just resist rules. They resist being shaped.

Rita shaped. Marcela shaped. Maggie tried not to hurt.

In a culture that increasingly frames discomfort as damage, shaping can look like harm. But so can its absence. A parent who never corrects never equips. A parent who never withholds approval never teaches how to self-generate it. Children need both truth and containment. Not because they're fragile. Because they're forming. And formation without shape is just exposure. All feeling. No frame.

Helplessness as Legacy

Helplessness doesn't announce itself. It settles in. Slowly. It hides behind gentleness, silence, and the quiet hope that things will work themselves out.

Maggie didn't pass down trauma. Her children weren't abused. They were excused. She passed down delay. She buffered them from failure, and downplayed responsibility. She was quick to soothe their sadness and frustration before they learned to carry it. Over time, Maggie's type of help became more than support. It turned into the only way they knew how to function. Eventually, that need defined how they saw themselves.

This shift, when help becomes habit, often goes unnoticed. The parent begins by responding to need. Then responding before need. Eventually, they anticipate it. The child learns they are safest when struggling. That comfort will arrive faster when they signal they may be in over their head. They learn if they fall apart soon enough by crying, shutting down, panicking, adults back off and they often skip accountability altogether.

Over years, that child may lose the natural impulse to get back up, keep going, or face what's hard. The resilience needed for everyday challenges is never learned because they were never required to build it.

It's tempting to see this as emotional overprotection, but the pattern runs deeper. Studies on intergenerational trauma show that stress responses, especially those tied to powerlessness, can be passed down biologically, not just emotionally. Rachel Yehuda's research on Holocaust survivor families revealed physiological stress markers in children and grandchildren who had never experienced the original trauma (Yehuda, 2001). Cortisol regulation, reactivity to threat, even baseline perceptions of safety were altered through chronic modeling, without any direct exposure.

This matters because the brain doesn't know the difference. Generational dysfunction isn't just a failure of discipline, it's a nervous system adapting to absence. When fear is passed down long after the threat is gone, vigilance becomes the default. The child doesn't know why they freeze or hold back. They've just absorbed the pattern.

Maggie didn't frighten her children, but she lived with a steady undertone of defeat. She had an arsenal of phrases for her powerlessness. "Some people just aren't built for more." "At least we survived." "The world's too fast now." Her children absorbed those phrases long before they knew what they meant.

They absorbed the tone first. The posture. The resignation in her breath when bills came due. The apology in her voice when a boundary slipped. The stories that ended before anything changed.

That kind of repetition builds identity.

To be formed by helplessness doesn't require abuse. It requires proximity to someone who has stopped trying, and who believes, at some level, that trying doesn't matter.

By contrast, formation grounded in effort, even amid chaos, creates different instincts. A child who watches a parent try again doesn't need the outcome to be perfect. They just need to see the loop completed. Feel the rhythm of recovery. Handle frustration without breaking down.

This is where the legacy splits: some were shown how to keep going. Others were left to figure it out as they went.

Children raised in chronically understructured homes often carry an invisible weight: the belief that life is too much for them. That others know something they don't. That some people just "have it", whatever it is, and they don't. They speak this belief in passing. In apology. In resignation.

"I'm just not good at things like that."

"My brain doesn't work that way."

"I get overwhelmed really easily."

They don't say it to manipulate. They say it to belong.

Sometimes, the culture reinforces them. Therapists validate. Schools accommodate. Friends empathize. Everyone responds to the signal: I can't.

Eventually, the child learns to name their limits more fluently than their potential. They may be praised for "knowing themselves." For being "in touch." But under that language is a growing script: low expectation is love.

That script has consequences.

I knew a boy named Eli, bright, curious, easy to like. The kind of kid adults described as "sensitive" before they ever called him capable. He forgot things constantly, small promises, half-finished chores, plans he'd agreed to and then let slide. He was always there, but somehow never fully in it.

He didn't act out. He didn't resist. He just slipped into the background, hiding behind unfinished tasks, vague apologies, and the soft cushion of perpetual grace.

I watched him over time, mostly from the margins. His parents were gentle. Protective. His father once told me, "He's always had a hard time with pressure. We just want him to know he's okay no matter what."

There's nothing wrong with that instinct. Every child deserves that kind of dignity. But Eli had absorbed more than reassurance. He'd come to believe that nothing was expected of him because he couldn't handle anything.

In that absence of demand, he was adrift with no compass and no course.

When he finally earned something worth noticing, the occasional A, Student-of-the-Month, he was surprised. As if no one had ever taught him that trying could lead to something new, something different, maybe even exciting, frightening, or even worthwhile.

That kind of confusion comes from a worldview built on underestimation.

Parents like Eli's are often deeply loving. Deeply tired. They want to protect their children from shame, from overwhelm, from falling apart. But in protecting them from those things, they often protect them from growth too.

They don't yet know how to say: You're loved. And you're capable.

That's the legacy most often missing.

We assume harm is what marks a child. But omission marks them too. The absence of challenge. The silence where standards should be. The delay that turns into identity.

When expectations vanish, children do not feel liberated. They feel misplaced. Unnamed. Still forming, but with no outline.

We think we've protected them. What we've done is leave them unshaped.

And eventually, they will teach that shape to someone else.

CHILDren anD THE ECHO Of ADULT ABDICaTION

Who's Really Leading?

On paper, it looks like any other rental on the block. A single-story home, tucked behind an overgrown bush and a sagging fence. Three generations live inside. No one's leading, but everyone's there.

Monica is thirty-eight. She works thirty hours a week at a fast-food chain, recently promoted to assistant manager. She tells people the raise made a difference, though the rent is still late and dinner is usually drive-thru. Her hours qualified as work. Her effort passed as trying. Barely.

Her oldest, Tyler, is twenty. He left school four years ago and hasn't done much since. No job. No school. No plans. He sleeps until noon, scrolls through videos, shrugs off suggestions. If asked to take out the trash, he'll do it three hours later, maybe. If reminded, he'll sigh, maybe grunt. He doesn't argue. He just doesn't act.

Then there's Jayden. Five years old. He doesn't listen, doesn't answer, doesn't stop. He runs, touches, interrupts, ignores. When spoken to, he keeps moving. When corrected, he escalates. His speech is limited, his attention fractured. Every room he enters becomes chaotic. When the volume gets too high, someone hands him a phone. The room goes quiet. Until the battery dies.

Monica doesn't shout. She rarely enforces. She tries to talk things down, reason softly, distract. If that fails, she withdraws. She scrolls through her own phone, complains to coworkers about how hard it all is, and buys herself small comforts, candles, throw pillows, seasonal snacks from the clearance aisle at Walmart. She says money's tight, but there's always something new in the cart.

The house is functional in the loosest sense. The fridge hums. The lights work. But nothing holds shape. There's no rhythm. No one cleans unless prompted. Dishes pile up. Repairs go unfixed until Monica calls her dad. Can you bring your ladder? Can you help patch this? Nothing gets done unless someone outside the house does it.

That someone, her father, used to be married to the woman who now lives in the back room.

Carmen, the grandmother, pays part of the rent from her disability check. Her room is tidy, newly painted, and rearranged twice a year, always by someone else. She doesn't own the house, but she treats her space as sacred. The rest is someone else's problem.

She dotes on Jayden. Says he's just spirited. Says he shouldn't be pushed. If he wants to run the room, let him. If he doesn't want to pick up after himself, that's fine. He's only five. When Monica sighs about being behind on bills, Carmen nods and changes the subject. Her rent is paid. The rest doesn't concern her.

Years ago, when Monica and her sons lived under Carmen's roof, things looked different. Carmen filed paperwork to collect back rent from her daughter. Called it fairness. Said adults should contribute. She had rules then. Standards. Consequences. Now she has comfort. And no memory of the standards she once enforced.

Carmen and Monica don't speak so much as clash. Their arguments flare quickly, accusations, complaints, shouting across rooms, and never resolve. Carmen criticizes how Monica runs the household. Monica fires back that if Carmen had done better herself, none of this would be happening. Neither backs down. Neither changes course. The fights reset like weather.

Tyler stays quiet during these exchanges. He's learned there's no upside to speaking. He retreats to his room, stews in silence, and tells anyone who will listen that he wishes his grandmother would just move out. Carmen, for her part, barely masks her contempt. She thinks Tyler's lazy, entitled, disrespectful, and says as much. She's fine being left alone.

Jayden, meanwhile, operates in a different atmosphere. Monica yells at him constantly. "Boy, I'm going to bust your ass," she says, or worse. The words escalate as her frustration builds. But the follow-through is rare. If she raises her voice, he ignores her. If she raises her hand, Carmen intervenes. And Jayden, sharp in his own way, knows the pattern. He keeps pushing until Monica physically gets up. Then, maybe, he stops.

The home doesn't feel abusive. It feels reactive. Loud, chaotic, emotionally saturated, but low on consequence. Rules are threatened but rarely enforced. Authority is performed, not embodied. Everyone is fighting someone, but no one is in charge.

Jayden learns to operate within that chaos. He tunes out what he doesn't fear. He registers only what moves. Tyler learns to disappear. Carmen protects her space. Monica fluctuates between complaint and collapse. And the home, slowly, becomes a place where nothing stabilizes, because no one was willing to hold the center.

This is what generational drift looks like up close. Not absence, but noise and volatility. It's not neglect in the traditional sense, but a loss of structure so complete that every interaction becomes a form of improvisation.

And the children adapt. Not toward growth, but away from it.

Fragility as a Baseline

Tyler hasn't left the house in six weeks.

He got his driver's license, finally, because his grandfather insisted. Not because he wanted the freedom, or had plans to use it, or saw it as a step toward independence. He didn't want to wait in line at the DMV. Didn't want to fill out paperwork. Didn't like the idea of being told what to do, even if it was a single appointment. But he finished it, because someone else made him.

Now it's done. The license sits in a drawer. And Tyler remains where he's always been, indoors, reclined, silent, scrolling. There are no obstacles left. No logistical reason he hasn't applied for work, made a call, or left the house. The barriers were never external.

They were internal. Or more precisely, they were never challenged to begin with.

This is what developmental fragility looks like in its quietest form. Not emotional collapse. Not panic or overwhelm. Just the absence of momentum. The absence of strain. A life lived so long without structure that effort feels foreign, optional, even offensive.

Fragility here doesn't mean easily hurt. It means easily stalled.

Jayden, at five, lives in a different stage of the same pattern. He is not shy or withdrawn. He is constantly in motion, but unmoored. When told no, he screams. When ignored, he escalates. He is not pushing boundaries, he is discovering that they don't exist. Or if they do, they come too late to matter.

His world is pure stimulus and response. There is no pause between feeling and action, no space between impulse and outcome. If he's loud enough, something gives. If he's wild enough, someone intervenes, with a phone, with a snack, with an empty threat.

This is not defiance in the moral sense. It's unformed wiring. Jayden has never had to hold tension, so he cannot. His nervous system is trained to chase the next input, and to avoid the stillness that makes discipline possible.

And when correction finally comes, it comes laced with volume, profanity, and performative threat. "I'm going to bust your ass" becomes a daily soundtrack. But Jayden knows the beats too well. Nothing happens until Mom stands up. If she doesn't move, he doesn't stop.

This pattern, escalate, warn, retreat, teaches a lesson more deeply than any lecture: there are no consequences, only crescendos.

Children like Jayden don't just lack self-regulation. They lack modeled regulation. And that difference matters. The skill isn't absent by default, it was never introduced through relationship.

This is fragility, too. Not fragility of emotion, but of development.

It's the kind that doesn't draw attention in the same way. It looks like laziness, apathy, or willful chaos. But underneath is a nervous system conditioned to chaos, a body wired to expect rescue or retreat instead of resilience.

No one in this household is modeling how to manage discomfort. They yell, defer, or disconnect. And so the children, one fully grown, one just beginning, learn that frustration is not to be worked through. It is to be waited out, until someone else shifts.

Resilience isn't built by being left alone. It is built through structured strain. That strain never arrived.

Tyler quit school at sixteen. Two years in Job Corps gave him some direction, but not enough to hold. No one in his house was charting a path. No one expected follow-through. He had time, options, even a government program invested in his success. But he didn't push forward, because nothing in his upbringing prepared him for sustained effort.

The outcome is not surprising. He doesn't fight against responsibility. He simply sees no point in it. This is what happens when a child never develops endurance. It's the result of low stakes and high indulgence. Because no one expected him to stretch, he never did.

Jayden is not far behind. At five, he should be learning the basics of pause, wait, listen. But his entire environment rewards immediacy. Attention is won with volume. Comfort arrives before consequence. There is no reward for trying again, only friction if he doesn't get what he wants.

What gets called "behavioral issues" are often just the outer symptoms of a nervous system that has never known how to slow down. Jayden doesn't calm because he doesn't know what calm feels like. He can only shut down, or speed up. The middle range, regulation, patience, recovery, was never introduced.

Fragility becomes the baseline, not because anyone chose it, but because no one corrected it.

This is the fragility of a child who was never asked to grow. A child whose tantrums were tolerated, whose demands were met, whose limits were barely tested. A child whose environment never pushed back, until life eventually will.

And when that push comes, it won't be delivered gently. School, work, relationships, each one has expectations that won't adjust downward. Jayden will not be five forever. Tyler isn't anymore.

But neither is equipped to respond to challenge without collapse, avoidance, or blame.

That's the cost of a structureless childhood. Not just disobedience. Not just delay. But a nervous system that cannot carry weight, and a mind that never learned how.

The Echo Chamber of Institutions

Tyler never had to fight the current of expectation, because there wasn't one. School made room for his disinterest. Job Corps gave him structure, but released him back into a life where no one noticed whether he used it. And now, with no school, no job, no demands, he is simply still.

Not stalled by barriers. Not paralyzed by fear. Just conditioned to stillness.

The institutions around him didn't push, they adjusted. They offered leniency, accommodation, second chances. Assignments could be late. Behavior was "expressive." Engagement was optional. Grades held less weight. Effort lost urgency. No one called it quitting. It was framed as self-paced, self-guided, "where he was at."

This isn't failure in the traditional sense. It's slow erosion. A classroom becomes a place to manage children, not form them. Feedback softens. Structure loosens. Standards float. The student doesn't rebel, he fades.

For Jayden, the process starts even earlier. Preschool settings now carry the language of wellness, but the practice is mostly containment. When he yells, the teacher kneels beside him, speaks softly, tries to calm the room. When he acts out or hits another child, the approach shifts, he's removed or sent home. The threat is lifted so the day can go on. The disruption ends, but nothing is learned.

But Jayden doesn't need peace in this sense. He needs anchoring. He's not wrestling with big emotions. He's rehearsing what it means to overpower a room. And each time the room bends, he learns something concrete, his behavior governs the environment. Not because he is strong, but because no one else is steady.

Teachers are not blind to this. Many carry deep instinct and hard-won wisdom. But they are hemmed in by systems that have blurred the line between empathy and enablement. Correction is now coded as harm. Authority is seen as aggression. Structure must be softened until no one feels confronted, even the child whose behavior is running the room.

In these settings, regulation is replaced by negotiation. Jayden doesn't learn how to come back to center. He learns that enough volume rearranges the world around him. Not just at home. Now at school too.

This pattern isn't limited to education. Therapeutic spaces often follow the same loop. A child like Tyler sits in a chair, describes his disinterest, names his lack of motivation, and is told he's being honest with his truth. No challenge. No stretch. Just reflection.

What Tyler needs is not shame. But neither is it endless echo.

He needs someone to press back, to name what has calcified. Not gently, but clearly. His stasis is not neutral. It's a developmental flatline. And mirroring it under the banner of compassion only seals it in place.

Daniel Siegel, writing on child neurodevelopment, notes that regulation forms through relationship, but not just any relationship. It requires consistent, grounded, non-reactive presence. Dysregulation in a parent leads to dysregulation in the child. The child doesn't find balance in reaction. He finds it in calm resistance (Siegel, 2015).

Our systems no longer resist. They conform.

And so Tyler learns that not trying is a valid state. Jayden learns that screaming is a tool. And the world bends to children who were never asked to stand.

None of this emerges from malice. It comes from fear, fear of offending, of appearing too harsh, of damaging a child's self-esteem. But esteem is not built through accommodation. It is built through capability. And capability can't form in a vacuum. It needs friction, feedback, and firm lines.

Those lines are disappearing.

We have reached a moment where institutional authority has grown self-conscious. Correction is seen as coercion. Direction sounds like dominance. And in that confusion, children are handed freedom before they've built the capacity to use it.

Jayden is still young. His story is unwritten. But every day that structure defers to his mood, every system that reinforces his right to interrupt instead of guiding him to relate, those moments don't pass. They form him.

CHILDREN AND THE ECHO OF ADULT ABDICATION

Jayden started school this year. Monica and Carmen already assumed it wouldn't go well. They talked openly about how teachers wouldn't be able to handle him. How they'd probably push for medication. Not support. Not strategy. Sedation. The fix was expected to be chemical, not behavioral, not structural, not relational. Just quiet him down.

The prophecy held. The fix came as predicted, in the form of a pill. The adults at home don't see it as failure. They see it as inevitable. Jayden doesn't need to change. The school does. Or the dosage does.

This is the echo chamber: a home with no structure, mirrored by a system with no spine. Together, they raise children who are not broken but under-built, fragile not because they are damaged, but because they were never asked to carry weight.

Screens as Surrogates, Silence as Strategy

Emotional Delegation

Some children learn that comfort speaks through voices. Others learn that it glows.

As emotional demands rise in modern families, many parents no longer respond with coregulation, an adult's steady nervous system anchoring the child's. Instead, they hand off that responsibility to a device. Screens become the stabilizer. The adult becomes the observer.

This exchange rarely begins with neglect. It begins with irritation. A child sobs for attention or out of frustration. The adult is already worn thin. They don't have the energy to soothe or the will to parent. The screen appears with perfect timing. It soothes instantly. It works.

In the moment, it feels like relief. In repetition, it becomes delegation.

Emotional labor, once held in breath, tone, posture, is now absorbed by programming. The screen doesn't flinch. It doesn't escalate. It offers regulation stripped of relationship. The parent isn't absent, but they're no longer leading.

Over time, this pattern shapes belief. The child learns what to expect from distress: distraction. Not attunement, not guidance, not repair. Just redirection. They stop turning toward people. They stop asking for presence. Their emotional cues shift from outward expression to internal rerouting. The absence of outbursts appears as growth. It isn't.

Some adults mistake silence for self-regulation. In reality, the child has learned to vanish.

Mara was nine when her mother first called her "low maintenance." She didn't throw fits, didn't cling, didn't complain. She played games quietly in her room for hours. Her mother described her as mature for her age. Relatives admired her calm. What they didn't see was the exchange that made it possible.

At four, Mara had cried easily. Loudly. She struggled with transitions, resisted sleep, demanded proximity. Her mother, already strained by a divorce, reached for screens to manage those moments. The habit grew. iPads during meals. Videos during meltdowns. Cartoons before bed. Mara stopped screaming. She started retreating.

By seven, she knew what calmed her. She stopped expecting anyone else to offer it. At school, she became compliant. At home, she became silent. Her mother believed the phase had passed.

The phase hadn't passed. It had hardened.

What Mara learned to suppress would reemerge years later as a young adult. She had outgrown tantrums, but she replaced them with sudden shutdowns. Ghosting friends. Emotional withdrawal. Relational collapse. Her regulation hadn't matured. It had migrated.

In many families, these stories go unnamed. The patterns feel benign. A quiet house. A peaceful dinner. A child who doesn't interrupt. The absence of conflict becomes the working definition of success.

One grandfather, watching his grandson on a tablet during a family visit, said quietly, "We used to hush kids with a look. Now we hush them with a screen." He wasn't longing for stricter discipline. He was describing a shift in emotional authority. One generation kept children in line through presence. The next keeps them quiet through input.

This is the hidden cost of emotional delegation. When we stop offering our nervous system to children, they seek replacement systems. The screen delivers regulation without contact. It calms the child but teaches nothing about how to hold tension, how to wait, how to come back.

Regulation outsourced too early becomes avoidance coded as composure.

The Loop That Trains Avoidance

Screens soothe. That is their design. But the relief they offer comes at a cost: the brain adapts to escape instead of effort. Discomfort is met with stimulus. Sadness, anger, boredom, fatigue, each one draws the same offer: press play.

For a developing brain, this creates a loop. The child feels distress. The screen delivers relief. The brain registers pleasure. Dopamine is released. Over time, the association strengthens. Screen equals calm. No screen equals tension.

This isn't an addiction in the dramatic sense, shaking hands, locked doors, broken trust. It's a slower tethering. The child's internal state becomes externally managed by a device designed to reward minimal effort with maximal stimulation.

The behavioral result is often praised. Quiet children. Easy transitions. Self-directed play. But beneath the surface, regulation hasn't developed. It's been hijacked.

In *Dopamine Nation*, psychiatrist Anna Lembke (2021) outlines the core dilemma of modern stimulation: the more we seek pleasure in concentrated bursts, the more we experience pain in the absence of it. The brain's balance tips. Over time, even minor stress feels unbearable without the relief loop.

For children, this process begins early. A child wakes agitated. A tablet appears. The child settles. A parent exhales. The behavior changes, but the system that drove it does not resolve. It resets, until the next cue.

What's reinforced is escape, not endurance.

This cycle repeats in patterns too subtle to interrupt. The child doesn't melt down. They request the device. They don't protest. They check out. In many households, this looks like regulation. What's happening is chemical conditioning. The brain learns that discomfort should not be tolerated. It should be soothed. Preferably through novelty.

Dopamine loves novelty. It spikes in response to new sounds, images, and feedback. Modern digital platforms offer an endless stream. Every swipe delivers possibility. Every notification simulates attention. Every scroll offers a small promise: "This next thing will feel better."

For a child already conditioned to equate boredom with distress, the screen becomes medicine. Not metaphorically, neurologically.

This pattern doesn't resolve as the child matures. It deepens. Tolerance for low-stimulation environments weakens. Classrooms feel slow. Meals feel empty. Relationships feel dull. The child isn't broken. Their brain has adjusted to a reward cycle too fast for ordinary life to match.

Lembke describes this as the dopamine deficit state. After repeated spikes, the brain begins to compensate by reducing its sensitivity to pleasure. What once felt exciting now feels neutral. What once soothed now barely registers. The user, child or adult, chases stronger input to reach the same baseline. More volume. More speed. More chaos.

The baseline changes. So does the threshold for effort.

Screens don't demand anything back. They offer regulation without resilience. No negotiation. No mutuality. No adaptation.

The user is the only emotional agent in the interaction. In that dynamic, children lose something irreplaceable: the practice of coexisting with another nervous system.

Relational life requires patience. A conversation may bore you. A sibling may frustrate you. A parent may say no. These moments create stress. Without a practiced tolerance, they feel unbearable.

In screen-shaped regulation, there is no lag between discomfort and relief. In relational life, there's often only the lag.

This gap, the pause between stress and solution, is where resilience forms. Without it, the child develops preference, not strength.

The long-term cost surfaces quietly. A teenager can't tolerate waiting. A young adult drops tasks that feel slow. A partner zones out mid-conflict. These aren't character flaws. They're adaptations to a system that replaced pacing with payoff.

The screen delivered comfort without contact. The brain complied.

Disconnection as Design

Disconnection doesn't always result from trauma. Sometimes it arrives as strategy.

In homes shaped by uncertainty, children don't always cry louder. Some disappear. They learn that their presence complicates things. Their voice feels disruptive. Their needs pull too hard on the people around them. Over time, quiet becomes currency.

SCREENS AS SURROGATES, SILENCE AS STRATEGY

At first, adults describe these children as easy. Self-entertained. Observant. Undemanding. The behavior is praised. The child adapts more deeply.

This kind of silence isn't a void. It's a structure. Lucas was ten the first time his teacher called him "resilient." His father had been laid off again. Tension in the house ran high. Lucas never asked for seconds at dinner, never complained about forgotten rides. He stayed in his room most evenings with his games. His mother said he was independent.

By sixteen, Lucas had learned exactly how much emotion the household could absorb, very little. Anger triggered shutdowns. Sadness triggered worry. Joy sometimes got ignored. His safest move was withdrawal.

He stopped mentioning problems at school. He figured them out or let them fail. When friends asked if things were okay at home, he changed the subject. His quiet became protective. By the time he left for college, his inner world had shrunk to fit the bandwidth of others.

He still called home every Sunday. The conversations were short. Everyone said he was doing fine.

Children like Lucas don't resist connection. They adapt away from it. They learn that to be visible is to create tension. And so they regulate themselves through control, entertainment, or silence. The screen becomes part of this system, not just as escape, but as refuge.

Disconnection grows efficient.

This is the part families rarely name. Screens don't just substitute for presence. They organize the home around disengagement. Fewer interruptions. Fewer eruptions. Fewer collisions. The household moves quietly, predictably. Input replaces interaction. When connection requires no effort, it also builds no capacity. Children no longer learn to read a sigh, interpret a pause, or adjust tone mid-sentence. The subtle skills of social life, timing, reciprocity, tension, go unpracticed. The child may feel socially fluent online. Offline, they lose fluency.

The home feels peaceful, but in reality, it has gone silent by design.

That design is reinforced everywhere. Schools limit correction. Social platforms personalize input. Workplaces adjust expectations. Emotional engagement becomes optional, even intrusive. Disconnection becomes normalized.

The cultural shift completes itself quietly. We start valuing comfort over contact. We stop asking children to stretch. We reward autonomy without testing its depth. The feedback loop flattens. No push. No pull. No growth.

The child, once coregulated through voice, eye contact, and shared tension, now moves alone. They manage themselves by avoiding themselves. They learn to function by not needing.

Eventually, they forget what it felt like to be shaped by another human being.

The cost won't show up in grades. It won't appear in a single crisis. It will emerge as relational thinness, a life structured to run without others, except through interface. A life low in mess, low in conflict, and low in depth.

This is not a crisis of broken families. It's a quiet result of families that stopped bumping into each other.

No raised voices. No slammed doors.

Just fewer doors opening.

PART III SYSTEMS THAT KEEP US SMALL

DISABILITY, DESPAIR, AND THE DISAPPEARING LINE

From Diagnosis to Identity

Ella has arthritis and adult-onset diabetes. Neither condition prevents her from functioning, but both give her a reason not to. She receives a disability check, qualifies for subsidized housing, and has learned how to stay eligible. Her life is built around the slow erosion of expectation.

She avoids doing anything that might imply capability. Doesn't carry grocery bags. Doesn't walk far. Turns down invitations, citing flare-ups. When her caseworker asks how she's managing, she emphasizes instability. "It's unpredictable," she says. "I have to be careful." She knows what language signals risk, and how to use it to secure extensions, deferments, and continued aid.

Those around her notice the pattern. Friends mention how she lights up when talking about her favorite shows, but always fades when asked to join an event. Neighbors recall the time she shuffled down the street to pick up her prescription, but said she couldn't manage a three-block ride to a part-time volunteer shift. Everything is framed around what she can't do. The story stays fixed. The script rehearsed.

Her pain is real. But it isn't what holds her back. What holds her is the life she's constructed around being perceived as incapable. The condition became the structure. Then the justification. Then the identity.

There's no drama in her posture. No overt demand. She's quiet. Measured. Sympathetic. Her needs are modest, but constant. She plays the part of the cooperative dependent, grateful, but passive. There's no talk of progress, only management. No ambition to regain ground, only vigilance to protect what she's been granted.

Over time, she has come to expect that her condition will carry the weight of her life for her. The check replaces ambition. The limitation becomes lens. Every opportunity is pre-filtered: Would this threaten my benefits? Would this change what people assume about me?

This isn't manipulation. It's adaptation. Ella learned early that any sign of improvement could trigger scrutiny. So she stopped trying. Stopped talking about good days. Stopped letting strength show. To keep what she had, she had to stay where she was.

And sometimes, survival isn't the only goal. Some sell their government food allowances. Others sell the medications they receive at low or no cost, painkillers, stimulants, sedatives, anything with street value. Some do it occasionally. Others make it routine. It's not a secret. It's common knowledge in certain neighborhoods, treatment centers, and online spaces. Dependence becomes a business model, and the system keeps paying out, rarely looking too closely.

This pattern repeats across conditions and communities. Manageable illnesses become lifelong income streams. Support systems, once built to restore stability, drift into permanent subsidy. You don't notice it all at once. You notice it when someone who could have recovered decides not to, and realizes they don't have to. Eligibility is guarded. Potential is forgotten. And keeping people stuck gets mistaken for mercy.

Psychologist Martin Seligman (1975) described learned helplessness as a response to uncontrollable conditions. When people come to believe their actions no longer change anything, they stop trying, even when new options appear. At some point, the loss stops looking like a phase and starts looking like a choice. In Ella's case, helplessness wasn't the product of trauma. It was the product of low-risk rewards. If standing still is safer than stepping forward, then standing still becomes the plan.

The system doesn't need fraud to fail. It only needs people to stop moving.

And once that happens, stillness hardens into personality. A diagnosis becomes a framework. Every interaction runs through it. Every decision filters through protection, not possibility. The narrative locks in place. Improvement feels risky because of what might be lost if capacity returns.

The body might heal enough to try. But the story won't allow it. And sometimes the story is easier to protect than the person.

The Danger of Endless Accommodation

Accommodation is meant to be temporary. A way to catch someone before they fall through the cracks. At its best, it preserves dignity and stabilizes crisis. But when crisis becomes lifestyle, the structure meant to lift instead becomes something people build their lives around.

Policies shift to meet rising demand. Eligibility criteria expand, especially around mental health. Conditions once seen as situational, grief, anxiety, low motivation, are now labeled as chronic. It doesn't take long for people to notice how the system responds. The language gets softer. Definitions stretch. Words like "discomfort," "overwhelm," and "triggered" find their way into forms once reserved for serious impairment. And as that drift continues, the process of qualifying becomes less about incapacity and more about presentation.

What once responded to need now organizes around it. Schools that used to challenge students to rise now pad difficulty with caveats. Agencies once tasked with stabilizing families now ration growth as if it's a luxury. Caseworkers no longer ask what a person might still be able to do. They ask what they're most afraid of. And policy follows fear.

A man applies for assistance, citing chronic fatigue. His diagnosis is vague. His demeanor is pleasant. He mentions that work stresses him. The intake coordinator, exhausted herself, enters the code that opens eligibility. She doesn't probe. She doesn't push. Not because she believes him, but because the system no longer rewards discernment.

In the classroom, a student repeatedly misses deadlines. The teacher has tools: tiered supports, collaborative plans, accommodation pathways. She uses them. But when the pattern repeats and no growth occurs, she no longer revises her approach. She revises the grade.

In the clinic, a therapist listens to the same refrain for six months. The client describes a stuck life, no job, no relationships, no plan. But the conversation loops around triggers, family history, self-soothing. Movement isn't introduced. Goals are postponed. Trauma, real or unresolved, becomes a resting place instead of a foundation for repair.

The therapist takes notes. "Client insight increasing." There is no insight. Just repetition.

This is not dereliction. It's drift. Systems, like people, tire of confrontation. They become mirrors for the most immobile client, student, patient. And once that standard sets, it's hard to dislodge. People learn what to say. What to avoid. How to emphasize just enough pain to delay review. Some start by telling the truth, but realize quickly that honesty doesn't guarantee support, consistency does. So they make their story consistent. Bleed out the progress. Drop the detail that might signal recovery. Highlight the symptom, bury the strength.

And yes, some lie.

They describe their depression as "completely debilitating," though they're out with friends by evening. They claim a flare-up, then run errands. They list themselves as unable to work, while taking under-the-table jobs. It's not always malicious. Often it's pragmatic. People sense how much effort it takes to prove they're better, and how much easier it is to stay sick on paper.

Systems aren't blind to this. But they're cautious. Reviews are slow. Investigations rare. No one wants to deny a claim and be wrong. So the incentives lean passive. The benefit of the doubt flows in one direction. And people respond to that drift, by standing still.

Even the language of those processing the claims begins to shift. Notes read: "Appears stable, but continues to report severe symptoms." "Expresses willingness to work, but no follow-through." Translation: We know they're not being honest. We're not going to say so. The risk is too high.

Eventually, the pattern becomes the policy. And the policy becomes the norm.

When systems begin to resemble the individuals they're meant to support, something essential is lost. Compassion without expectation becomes collusion. Softness without direction becomes its own kind of sabotage.

We are told this is care. It isn't. Care is active. Care remembers who someone could be, not just who they are in the moment. Systems that care enough to provide must also care enough to invite strength. If that invitation never comes, what they're offering isn't support, it's sedation.

Students with mild symptoms receive testing accommodations. Adults with stable conditions qualify for disability. Emotional fatigue, once addressed with rest, now secures long-term deferral.

The intent may still be care, but the impact is often drift.

Support systems rarely revisit assumptions. Instead of restoring function, they maintain the present. Progress is no longer the goal. Stability is. And even that is defined loosely, as the absence of escalation, not the return of agency.

When discomfort is framed as danger, the safest path is to stop moving. People avoid anything that might threaten their narrative of limitation. They decline opportunities that require effort. They learn what language signals risk, and how to use it fluently. Over time, what began as a temporary pause is absorbed into the system. Inertia becomes procedure.

No one wants to be the one to challenge this. Educators fear accusations of insensitivity. Employers hesitate to question claims. Clinicians, pressed for time, affirm what they cannot re-evaluate. Even families tread carefully. If someone says they are too overwhelmed to try, pressing them further can be framed as harm.

So the language softens. The structure bends. And the expectation quietly disappears.

This is how helplessness becomes policy. And policy becomes identity.

The danger isn't fraud. It's inertia. Relief, left unchecked, replaces growth. When systems guarantee protection but ask nothing in return, the individual begins to match that design. They internalize the lowered bar. They adapt to the absence of pressure. And eventually, they stop imagining anything else.

Despair begins to surface, not as crisis, but as resignation. Not loud, not visible. Just a slow dulling of will. A soft agreement to stay in place.

Seligman's theory of learned helplessness describes this collapse. When people experience conditions where effort no longer yields results, they stop trying, even when new opportunities arise. In this model, helplessness isn't a personality flaw. It's a learned state, shaped by consistent exposure to non-contingent outcomes.

In today's systems, that exposure comes through protection. When effort is decoupled from expectation, people stop developing the capacity to push forward. They may not appear panicked or unstable. They are just still. Still in the same apartment. Still under the same label. Still repeating the same lines.

Relief becomes routine. Routine becomes identity. And inside that routine, despair lingers as a weight no one mentions. A kind of grief for what might have been, had someone asked more of them. Had they asked more of themselves.

Strategy by Standing Still

Some families do not simply tolerate dependence. They model it. Teach it. Protect it. In those homes, expression always outranks execution. The child learns to narrate their fears but not to face them. To name their blocks, but not to push through them. By adolescence, they speak with the fluency of the over-therapized and the stamina of the unformed. The phrase "that's too much for them" becomes shorthand for every avoided task. The parent doesn't step back. They step in. They accommodate until all expectation fades. The result is not closeness, but covert resentment. Because at some point, someone realizes they've been preparing their child not for life, but for dependence.

That realization comes too late, or not at all. And when it does, it is often buried in guilt, then passed to the next generation.

Some people don't just fall behind. They stay there, long after the reason for staying has passed. What begins as a collapse becomes the shape of their life. A setback turns into a story. The language hardens. They talk about being overwhelmed, broken, too far gone. They use phrases that signal caution and disarm confrontation. Over time, describing themselves this way becomes easier than testing whether it's still true. They build around that version of themselves because it works. They're treated carefully. Their burdens are affirmed. No one asks them to try.

I knew a woman once, family, extended. Her life unraveled after her husband was arrested. Four kids. No stability. She latched on to the first man who would have her. Then another. Worse followed. The spiral didn't take long. She lost her children. Protested loudly. Accused the courts, the system, everyone but herself. That was over a decade ago. She still leads with that story. Still points to it as the reason she can't move forward. The tragedy became her alibi. Protest was her only forward motion.

People used to worry. Now they mostly avoid her. It's not that they don't care. They've seen what happens when they try. She lashes out, reverts, replays the same grief for the same attention. She cries when she's ignored and lashes out when she's not. If no one helps, she gets louder. If someone does, she folds. Nothing changes. So they step back. Quietly. Permanently. They've learned there's no way in that doesn't cost too much to maintain.

In families, this kind of collapse breeds avoidance. Not polite concern, avoidance in every form. Calls go unanswered. Invitations stop. Plans are made without her in mind. Sympathy gave out years ago. Fatigue replaced it.

At first, there were attempts. Discussions. Explanations. Warnings. Ultimatums. But the message was always lost. She wasn't listening. She never stayed long enough in a conversation to hear anything that asked her to change. She whined when ignored, exploded when confronted, and accused when boundaries were set. Whatever door was opened, she slammed shut.

Now, there's no door at all. Only her father still tried. He told himself there was hope. That maybe this time would be different. He helped her apply for public assistance, drove her to appointments, helped fill out the paperwork, participated in calls. Once she was accepted, she disappeared. She stopped answering his calls and blocked him entirely. The help became a wall. The system replaced the family. And she's stayed there ever since.

What followed was silence. It was resignation. She isn't sensitive. She's unreachable. And eventually, people stop shouting across a chasm that never answers back.

This is what happens when a story is never interrupted. The role gets rehearsed until no one can imagine her playing anything else. Including her.

There's despair under it, but it isn't driving the behavior. What drives it is preservation, of control, of attention, of a carefully constructed identity that makes effort feel like threat. The fear is being asked to give up the one thing that still keeps people responding.

When that arrangement holds, everything else stalls. Effort disappears. So does accountability. She stays still, and eventually, everyone else learns to keep their distance.

She isn't fragile in the literal sense, but she has made fragility her only form of leverage. The pattern doesn't end with her.

Ella didn't need to break the system. She just learned how to survive inside what was already broken. So did others. The system stopped drawing the line. And the rest of us followed, slowly, as the gap between capacity and expectation widened until nothing in it made sense.

We didn't name the slide. We gave it new language. Then we funded it. Shared it. Made room for it: in policy, in parenting, in personality.

Now the line is a memory. A rumor from another time.

The kind of thing you heard older people mention, back when trying still meant something.

THE PERFORMANCE OF POWERLESSNESS

Helplessness as Social Capital

Helplessness no longer signals crisis. Increasingly, it signals credibility.

Visible suffering has become a shortcut to belonging, a substitute for resilience, and a viable strategy for social positioning. In a world that rewards emotional display over internal fortitude, collapse has evolved into a form of connection, offering not just relief from pressure, but prestige within particular cultural circles.

This shift is most visible in the way trauma is now styled and performed, especially across social media platforms like TikTok. The medium rewards curated vulnerability: tearful videos, whispered disclosures, and public breakdowns stylized to appear raw but timed for maximum reach. Posts tagged under mental health, trauma recovery, and self-care often drift into performative collapse, where the act of exposing distress substitutes for the work of actual recovery.

The style is recognizable. Soft lighting. Halting speech. Emotional unraveling presented in palatable, visually curated slices. Crying in a car becomes not an incidental low point, but an expected chapter of personal narrative. Distress, once something to move through, becomes something to hold up and share repeatedly, accruing views and validation with each performance.

The incentives are clear. Platforms reward engagement. Audiences reward relatability. Algorithms push content that evokes immediate emotional reaction. Recovery, with its slower, quieter trajectory, does not trend. What gains visibility is the moment of collapse, frozen in digital amber and broadcast for public consumption.

Curated vulnerability offers real connection, but of a narrowed kind. It forms bonds around unhealed wounds rather than earned growth. In this new attention economy, perseverance becomes invisible while collapse becomes the shared language of intimacy.

This phenomenon does not exist solely online. It reflects broader cultural shifts offline as well. In relationships today, emotional presence means something different. It's measured less by who stays steady through difficulty, and more by who can publicly inhabit fragility. The person who can articulate their suffering eloquently often holds more social gravity than the person who silently endures and recovers.

Historically, emotional presence was demonstrated through reliability, consistency, and strength in hardship. Today, presence is increasingly equated with exposure, the rawer the better. Those who expose the most win the right to define group norms, emotional climates, and even social hierarchies.

The rise of the fragile narrator is not simply the rise of storytelling about pain. It is the cultural privileging of unresolved pain as identity. Stories are no longer valuable because they move toward change; they are valuable because they vividly display suffering. The narrator's authority is anchored not in perspective gained, but in harm survived, preferably harm that remains fresh, unprocessed, and frequently revisited.

This cultural pattern shifts the dynamics of belonging. Rather than being invited into community through shared values, people are increasingly invited through shared collapse. Relatability is indexed through vulnerability, but the kind of vulnerability that asks nothing of the witness beyond validation. Growth, resilience, and quiet recovery do not generate the same gravitational pull.

There's a quieter cost inside this shift, the way effort itself begins to look suspicious. People who move forward too quickly, who heal without showing their process, are often seen as cold, even disloyal to the unspoken pact of shared hurt. What began as solidarity turns into a place to stay.

Social theorist Pierre Bourdieu (1986) described forms of capital, economic, social, cultural, that structure the distribution of power in society. Today, we see a new form emerging: trauma capital. It operates much like cultural capital but is accrued through the currency of suffering. Those who possess visible, narratable wounds gain access to sympathy, moral authority, and protective concessions. The uninjured, or those who conceal their injuries, find themselves increasingly marginalized in emotional economies that prize fragility.

Helplessness as social capital erodes the value of resilience while incentivizing the public maintenance of pain. It pressures individuals not simply to share their hardships, but to remain in them visibly and indefinitely. Movement away from collapse becomes not a triumph, but a risk, one that may sever community ties, diminish audience engagement, or weaken social standing.

The long-term result is predictable. The cultural narrative shifts from "we struggle and overcome" to "we struggle and are seen." Endurance becomes a private act, stripped of communal resonance. Collapse becomes a public performance, richly rewarded but quietly corrosive.

What begins as an earnest attempt to destigmatize emotional hardship slides into the creation of fragile identities built on constant self-exposure. Pain stops being a passage and becomes a platform.

And when helplessness becomes a form of credibility, recovery becomes an act of disappearance.

When Suffering Becomes Influence

In an earlier era, social influence was anchored in achievement, contribution, or personal transformation. Today, it is increasingly anchored in exposure. The more visible one's wounds, the greater their perceived authenticity, and by extension, their authority. This new architecture of influence rewards public suffering over private resilience.

This cultural economy functions much like Bourdieu's earlier frameworks: social and cultural capital once derived from trust or education. Today, visibility of pain carries its own form of capital, victimhood, conferring status, insulation from critique, and moral authority.

Victimhood capital functions like other forms of capital: it confers advantages. Individuals who present themselves as survivors of trauma, especially trauma that remains open, active, and narratively compelling, often find themselves elevated in social, professional, and digital spaces. Their experiences grant them a form of moral authority that insulates against criticism and elevates their voice within group dynamics.

This system is not always malicious or manipulative. In many cases, it is intuitive. Individuals disclose pain to seek solidarity, not power. Yet over time, the reward structures surrounding disclosure begin to shape behavior. The people who share their suffering most openly, or in the most vivid ways, often receive the greatest sympathy. The ones who stay composed, who heal without a public story, tend to fade from view.

Online, the contrast grows sharper. Platforms like TikTok, Instagram, and X push personal narratives of trauma faster than almost anything else. Videos tagged with #mentalhealth, #trauma, or #selfcare often outperform even highly curated lifestyle content.

Emotional breakdowns presented through stylized vignettes, tears, dissociation, whispered confessionals, move faster than stories of recovery or perseverance.

The performance code is subtle but clear. Pain must remain vivid. Movement toward healing must be slow or, at times, absent. Users who demonstrate visible struggle without offering resolution maintain engagement. Those who "heal too quickly," or who transition their content toward stability, often report losing followers, sponsorships, or algorithmic reach.

The social expectation shifts: continue suffering, or vanish.

This dynamic produces a difficult tension. Real pain is often present. Real struggle is undeniable. Yet the cultural framework that rewards unresolved trauma creates a pressure to remain visibly broken. Healing risks irrelevance.

Influencers who build audiences around curated vulnerability often face a paradox. If they move toward recovery, they lose the emotional intimacy that fueled their rise. If they stay frozen in collapse, they retain relevance but at the cost of growth. The audience, trained to consume pain, quietly resists closure.

This pressure is not limited to digital figures. It filters downward into ordinary relationships. A friend who consistently shares their distress may find themselves given more emotional space, less expectation, more social gravity. Another friend, who processes hardship privately and emerges quietly stronger, may become peripheral, less discussed, less needed, even less believed.

Victimhood capital operates by redistributing emotional credibility toward the visibly wounded and away from the quietly recovering. Over time, the cultural suspicion of effort, endurance, and personal repair grows. We come to trust those who expose, not those who endure.

At scale, the implications are profound. Narratives of struggle become central to personal identity, not as a chapter of growth, but as a credential in themselves. The social scaffolding built to honor and recognize suffering slowly hardens into an architecture that demands it.

One viral example illustrates the point: a young woman, previously a mental health advocate on TikTok, shifted her content over a year from personal breakdowns to gradual narratives of recovery, therapy progress, lifestyle changes, emotional resilience. Her viewership dropped by 70%. Engagement plummeted. Comments turned cold. Accusations surfaced that she had become "unrelatable." Within months, she reverted to posting tearful, fragmented videos. Her engagement recovered immediately.

The audience did not want her better. They wanted her broken.

This is the hidden performance code of our era: remain open-ended, remain wounded, remain consuming sympathy without resolution.

The tragedy is not that vulnerability has become more visible. Visibility matters. The tragedy is that vulnerability without movement has become idealized, even required. Authentic recovery, which demands discomfort, delayed gratification, and sustained effort, loses cultural resonance.

We are not merely validating struggle. We are rewarding immobility.

Over time, the emotional climate grows brittle. Encouragement sounds like betrayal. Challenge feels like abandonment. Those who attempt to push forward become suspect, accused of erasing their "true self" or minimizing the realities of pain.

And so the architecture of influence tilts ever further toward the fragile, the unfinished, the perpetually recovering.

This is not an indictment of those who suffer. It is a reckoning with the culture that has made suffering a station to occupy, rather than a place to pass through.

Until the currency of collapse loses its value, real recovery will remain countercultural.

Who Absorbs the Cost

Every system that privileges fragility must find someone to carry the load it no longer demands of the vulnerable. The burden doesn't disappear. It redistributes, quietly, unevenly, and almost always onto the most stable shoulders available.

In families, workplaces, and social systems built around emotional concession, a pattern emerges: the strong absorb what the weak refuse to carry. The dependable family member who handles crises without complaint. The employee who covers for the overwhelmed coworker. The friend who listens endlessly but never interrupts. These individuals become the invisible infrastructure of relational life, the ones who make systems appear functional even as they sag under the weight of chronic collapse.

This form of emotional taxation rarely announces itself. It accumulates slowly, over years, until exhaustion hardens into resentment. The "strong one" becomes less available, not out of cruelty, but out of depletion.

In family systems, the dynamics are often clearest. A struggling sibling falls apart during minor stressors. Their issues dominate conversations, planning, and emotional bandwidth. Parents recalibrate their expectations downward, reorganizing family life around crisis avoidance. Meanwhile, the stable sibling is expected to require nothing. Their success becomes invisible, their needs secondary, their resilience mistaken for infinite capacity.

Over time, the message is clear: collapse commands attention; stability does not.

The emotional cost compounds. Stable individuals learn that strength earns silence, not support. Their milestones are under-celebrated. Their challenges are minimized. Their crises, when they occur, are met with confusion or even irritation, "you're the strong one; you'll figure it out."

A similar burden emerges in professional environments. Teams with one or two emotionally volatile members often recalibrate around fragility. Deadlines flex. Accountability softens. Managers, reluctant to risk an emotional spiral, redirect tasks to more reliable employees. Stability becomes a curse: more work, more tolerance, less recognition.

The workplace stable ones rarely protest. They sense the unwritten contract: your resilience is expected, not celebrated. Fragility gets negotiated; competence gets exploited.

Over time, fatigue sets in. It's not dramatic depletion, but a quiet erosion of motivation. The emotionally responsible begin to ask themselves, often silently, why they are working harder for fewer returns. Some leave. Some harden. Some disengage internally while maintaining outward appearances. The emotional cost doesn't explode; it leaks.

The watchers, the ones who carry, experience a particular kind of grief. They grieve the quiet loss of mutual effort, the fading of relationships that once felt reciprocal, the erosion of norms that used to honor striving. More than anything, they wonder whether their endurance ever truly mattered.

In Bourdieu's (1986) terms, the emotional capital of the steady ones loses value over time inside systems that prize fragility. Their steadiness no longer brings respect or influence. It just keeps the system running. They become background characters, reliable, necessary, but invisible, carrying the emotional arcs of others while losing track of their own.

This quiet redistribution of emotional labor leaves its own casualty: the steady ones who hold everything together until there's nothing left to hold them. Those who maintain family holidays, uphold team performance, sustain friendships through unbalanced seasons. Their efforts hold systems together, but their fatigue unravels privately.

Emotional exhaustion isn't the only consequence. Rescuers and carriers often delay their own development. They postpone ambitions, friendships, and risks, sacrificing personal growth for relational stability. They learn to expect less, to need less, to want less.

And still, the system pulls for more.

No amount of carrying ever restores balance. As fragility accrues power, expectations of stability only deepen. The emotionally responsible are asked, implicitly or explicitly, to absorb not just tasks and tensions, but also the collective guilt for failing to "save" those who remain collapsed.

Over time, this creates a moral fatigue. The stable ones begin to doubt their own goodness, resenting both the burden and their own bitterness. They question why their efforts feel increasingly futile, why their presence feels increasingly taken for granted, and why escape feels increasingly impossible.

Some withdraw, emotionally if not physically. Relationships maintained through endurance rather than mutuality slowly fray. Teams built on silent compensation slowly bleed their strongest members. Family systems designed around the most fragile eventually hollow out, leaving only ritualized concern and chronic disappointment.

The cultural cost of sustaining fragility is not just the erosion of individual will. It is the corrosion of collective resilience.

When the emotionally responsible reach their threshold, and they always do, the collapse they have delayed becomes harder, sharper, more lasting. Their exit, whether physical, emotional, or relational, often catches others by surprise. Accustomed to their strength, others fail to notice the slow leaks until the final breach.

And in the aftermath, the system must finally reckon with a truth it has spent years denying: someone was always carrying more than their share.

The architecture of helplessness cannot sustain itself. It relies on steady shoulders that grow tired long before they grow loud.

When those shoulders finally drop their load, the reckoning is not immediate. It is slow, quiet, and costly.

Because the ones who carried never announced the weight until they laid it down.

Dreams Without Work
The Myth of the Lucky Escape

Passive Fantasy in Modern Culture

There is a quiet shift happening in how people imagine their futures. In place of practice, they wait. Not out of laziness, but calculation. They believe the system rewards the lucky, the visible, or the wronged. So they stop building, and begin hoping for a break, for an offer, for someone to fix the conditions they do not feel equipped to face.

This is not only wishful thinking. It is strategy, shaped by systems that have increasingly made consistency irrelevant and grievance profitable. Hard work may still be admired in theory, but fewer people expect it to pay off. The more visible path now begins not with effort, but with selection. Someone notices. Something changes. You are lifted. Exempted. Rewarded without being proven.

Lottery culture has made this explicit. What used to be a once-a-week gamble is now a worldview. People don't just buy tickets. They count on them. They watch others win gameshow prizes, settlement payouts, viral monetization, and they hold space for the idea that their turn is coming. Retirement depends on luck. Eliminating debt depends on luck. A home, a business, a second chance, all possible if something hits.

This isn't limited to gambling. The lottery has been absorbed into the cultural bloodstream. It shows up in social media strategies, where visibility is mistaken for viability. It shows up in the idea that you don't need to climb, just go viral. You don't need to produce, you just need to be discovered. The world is filled with people stockpiling dreams and waiting for recognition that may never arrive.

Litigation culture feeds the same impulse. The belief that someone else caused the delay. That the injury is external, and compensation is owed. The logic is not always wrong. There are real harms and real redress. But the strategy is increasingly normalized. Harm is positioned not just as a wrong to be righted, but as an asset. In some circles, being offended is a form of leverage. In others, it's the only power left.

The trend isn't just legal. It's social, professional, and personal. Employees file complaints to secure exits. Students allege trauma to avoid consequence. Influencers build brands around betrayal. The pattern is consistent: pain becomes currency, and systems reward it.

Over time, this shifts how people approach struggle. They don't try to outgrow it. They learn to present it. If hardship can pay, resolution becomes loss. If the system rewards stuckness, movement looks like surrender. There is less incentive to get better when attention, protection, or validation depend on staying unwell, under-resourced, or emotionally injured.

You hear it in passing, at the grocery store, at the county clerk's office, outside the gas station. A man grumbles about prices, says he can't afford new tires, then spends twenty dollars on scratch-offs. Another turns down a job "on principle," says he's holding out for a settlement after someone tapped his bumper in a Walmart parking lot. The lawyer says it could be big. Until then, he's not risking his eligibility.

These aren't stories of laziness. They're strategies. Quiet calculations shaped by a culture where effort rarely moves the needle, but luck might. Each person is waiting on a check, a win, a payout that will lift them out of the slow grind they no longer trust to lead anywhere.

The self-help industry sells a different version of the same equation. Programs offer wealth through alignment, love through self-image, and purpose through visualization. These aren't fringe beliefs. They're mainstream narratives, reinforced by media and language that celebrate wanting without demanding discipline.

It sounds personal, even empowering. But the effect is numbing. Effort becomes pathology. Struggle is evidence of resistance.

The more someone tries, the more they are told they are doing it wrong. If results don't appear, it's not because the work is hard, it's because their mindset is misaligned. The same culture that mocks lottery buyers tells people to manifest abundance through better energy.

The outcome is the same. It removes effort from the equation. What matters is readiness, not labor. What determines outcome is how cleanly you believe, not how consistently you build. The person who posts about growth is affirmed more than the one who pursues it quietly and without audience.

This has created a generation of performers, not practitioners. People who curate progress, hint at transformation, and outsource accountability. They are not without desire. They just no longer trust effort to take them where they want to go.

The cultural scaffolding has changed. Systems now orient themselves around claims, not capacity. Institutions track injury more carefully than endurance. The person who adapts is expected to carry the load. The person who collapses is asked what they need.

And so more people collapse. Not dramatically, but subtly. They reduce ambition to comfort. They reframe discomfort as dysfunction. They reject incremental growth as oppressive. In doing so, they trade possibility for positioning.

This is not a crisis of character. It is a shift in incentives. Over time, effort becomes eccentric. Accountability looks aggressive. The idea of changing through challenge is replaced by the hope of being recognized, rewarded, or rescued before the hard part begins.

In the space where growth used to live, fantasy blooms. Not childish or wild, but curated and plausible. Someone wins the settlement. Someone meets the right person. Someone is scouted, shared, or saved. Why not you?

The belief is quiet, but persistent: stay visible, stay sympathetic, stay available for the break. In a world where systems reward grievance, proximity, or luck, it no longer feels naive to wait. It feels smart.

No one says this out loud, but they live it.

And increasingly, they teach it.

Media compounds this. Old stories of destiny, the orphan prince, the hidden heir, are repackaged through screens. The teenager who sings into a hairbrush, then signs a record deal. The barista discovered by a director. The young woman who wakes up viral.

The message is smooth: you will be lifted, not built. Someone will see you. Someone will select you.

Children grow up narrating their lives in this frame. College graduates imagine being found online. Artists post portfolios, not to hone their craft, but to be anointed.

There is no training montage. No apprenticeship. Only waiting.

And waiting demands hope. But hope without agency grows sour. Eventually it shades into resentment: why her, not me? What energy did I fail to summon?

Zeynep Tufekci (2015) observed that viral fame often collapses lives precisely because it is unearned. Those propelled by it rarely have the infrastructure, emotional or practical, to absorb the change. Overnight attention is not the same as built capacity. What flashes brightly often burns through.

Viral success without scaffolding is a cruelty disguised as fortune.

Yet the fantasy persists. It offers something ambition cannot: absolution from effort. Permission to be chosen instead of made.

The modern economy has perfected the illusion of escape. Not from poverty alone, but from process. From patience. From being one among millions working quietly, unrewarded. It replaces the climb with the jump. The long road with a platform. The slow build with a breakout.

Something for Nothing

The dream is familiar: leave your job, skip the grind, earn six figures from your phone. Freedom sold as a download. Wealth bundled into a course. All for one low fee.

Affiliate marketing is the most common gateway. Post a link, earn a commission. The model promises passive income from passive action, promote someone else's product, automate everything else. Success stories flood TikTok and YouTube. A 19-year-old claims to have made $40,000 in a month. A stay-at-home parent shows receipts. A man with no experience says ChatGPT built his entire dropshipping empire in a weekend.

What's sold is not a product. It's detachment. The idea that profit is now decoupled from creation. That you can be the middleman, the signal-booster, the lifestyle brand, and the money will follow. You don't need to know the item. You don't need to believe in it. Just set up the funnel, use the template, follow the steps. If you fail, it's not the model, it's you. You didn't scale fast enough. You didn't "stay hungry." You treated it like a side hustle instead of a mindset.

The same dream powers Amazon FBA and dropshipping schemes. No inventory, no employees, no expertise. Just find a product, push it to market, and outsource the rest. Gurus show dashboards with $300,000 in monthly sales, recorded from a beach. They never mention the ad spend, the customer complaints, the refund rates, the accounts frozen overnight.

The appeal is obvious. You're told to act like a founder without having to become one.

This dream of instant ascent continues in the influencer economy. Millions now try to convert daily life into monetized performance. Personalities become products. Children learn to narrate themselves by age six. Teenagers track engagement metrics like heart rates. Young adults sell access to their identity, their aesthetic, their breakdowns, anything that gains reach.

The promise is always the same: "Just be you. Post consistently. Find your niche. The algorithm will find you."

The effort appears low. Talk to the camera. Share your day. Tag the right brand. Millions do this every day, chasing visibility not as a means, but as an end. To be seen is to be viable. To go viral is to be validated.

What's hidden is the backend: the management, the edits, the pressure to escalate. Most never break even. Some burn out from performance fatigue. Others buy fake followers just to stay in the game. But still, the belief persists: if I just show up, something might happen.

Virality is framed as a democratic miracle. In truth, it is a gamified lottery with moving targets and rigged odds.

Crypto promised a different escape. Not through content or conversion, but through asymmetry. The early buyer wins. The person who "did the research." The one who saw what others missed. Bitcoin millionaires made the story real enough to sell. So did Dogecoin, NFTs, meme coins built in an afternoon that soared and collapsed before most people could find the sell button.

What mattered wasn't understanding. It was timing. The dream was that money could be made from nothing but attention. From being early. From guessing right.

The same logic now powers retail trading platforms that gamify options and forex. One viral post shows a user turning $300 into $12,000 in a week. He shares screenshots. He sells access to his private chat. He offers mentorship for a price.

What isn't shown is that most users lose everything. Not from fraud, but from volatility. The entire model depends on people confusing motion for mastery. They believe wealth is a matter of rhythm, not rigor.

These aren't scams in the traditional sense. They are systems that sell permission. Permission to skip apprenticeship. Permission to monetize personality. Permission to believe you are one tactic away from everything changing.

It isn't greed that draws people in. It's erosion. Trust in slow success has collapsed. Few believe in the ladder anymore. They just hope for a rope.

And so they try. Not with steady hands, but with desperation masked as ambition. They buy the program. They start the store. They upload the pitch. They open the app. Not because they are lazy, but because they have been told that effort is optional now. That someone, somewhere, is getting rich doing less.

Maybe this time, it's you.

The Myth of Escape

For every story of overnight wealth, there are millions who quietly return to their jobs, delete the app, or abandon the login. Most never talk about it. The failure feels personal. They didn't "manifest" hard enough. They missed the trend. They posted the wrong day. They bought the wrong coin.

But the failure isn't personal. It's structural. The promise was never built to scale.

The modern escape strategy is a high-volume funnel: the more people who try, the better the model works, for someone. Platforms profit from every click, every attempt, every desperate sprint toward sudden gain. The few who win become advertisements. The rest are data.

What's sold is hope, cheap, fast, and constantly refreshed. But the cost comes later. When effort has been bypassed for too long, the muscles that carry growth atrophy. People forget how to improve. They forget what improvement even feels like.

Instead of asking what they want to build, they ask why they haven't been chosen.

Instead of practicing, they brand.

Instead of failing small and early, they wait for a high-stakes break, and when it doesn't come, they fall harder.

The allure is easy to understand. These models remove friction. They strip away hierarchy. They tell you credentials don't matter, only confidence. That you are already enough. That trying harder is outdated thinking from a dying world.

It sounds like freedom. But it functions more like sedation.

Once effort is framed as pathology, resistance, self-sabotage, limiting beliefs, there's nowhere left to go. Struggle becomes failure. Delay becomes defeat. Any attempt to apply discipline is seen as a sign that you still don't "get it."

This inversion trains people out of resilience. They don't quit because it's hard. They quit because it's not instant. Anything less than exponential feels like insult.

Over time, the pursuit of easy success produces something worse than failure: inertia. A long-term disorientation about what's worth doing, what's real, what builds.

Some keep chasing the next opportunity, new niche, new platform, new pitch. Others stop trying altogether. They say they're burned out, but they've never endured real burn. They're scattered. Shamed. Paralyzed by the weight of too many almosts.

And beneath all of it, the world continues to demand something different. Employers still want consistency. Relationships still require investment. Rent still comes due. Markets still move.

The difference is that fewer people arrive equipped to meet it. What happens next is institutional. Schools lower standards to keep students engaged. Workplaces extend grace, but stop promoting. Agencies and nonprofits absorb what used to be learned through life. Government steps in where family and community used to offer ballast.

This redistribution is not always wrong. But it comes at a cost. Every time systems absorb individual instability, they teach the public that the need for scaffolding is permanent. That the absence of structure is not temporary, but inevitable. That someone will catch you, not just once, but as a way of life.

The long arc of this belief is not collapse. It's drift. A slow disengagement from the habits that used to hold culture together: contribution, apprenticeship, iteration. These are replaced by anticipation, grievance, and spectacle.

We see it in media. In politics. In the labor force. We feel it in relationships and institutions that once relied on shared effort but now bend to accommodate chronic passivity. The cultural center of gravity shifts, from builders to bypassers.

It's not a matter of intelligence. Most of these strategies require enormous creativity, energy, and even courage, at first. But they don't teach longevity. They don't build wisdom. They front-load hope and back-load disillusionment.

And when the disillusionment comes, it's hard to name. Because the system never said it would be fair, only that it could happen. That possibility is the hook. It keeps people compliant, grateful, always almost-there.

The tragedy is not in the chase. It's in what is lost while chasing: attention span, endurance, clarity, a working sense of cause and effect.

People who once wanted to grow become people who only want to escape. And when escape fails, there's no narrative left.

Because the old path, slow, steady, anonymous, now feels like punishment. They weren't trained to walk it. They were trained to be lifted.

And so they wait. For another offer. Another opening. Another way out.

But life is not a loophole.

It never was.

PART IV THE ROAD WE'RE WALKING

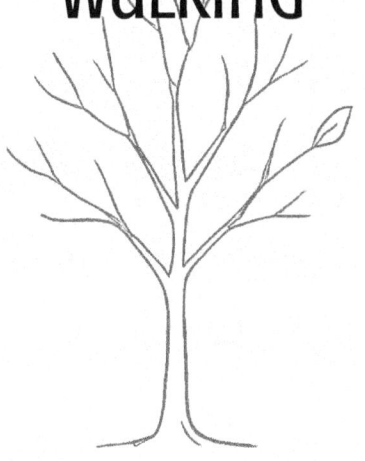

PART 1 THE ROAD WE'RE
WALKING

From Survival to Surrender
The Cultural Tipping Point

When Struggle Stops

Struggle is supposed to move. Even when it drags, even when it wounds, its direction is forward. But at some point, for some people, the direction stops mattering. The fight itself becomes a condition. Exhaustion settles in and redefines who they are.

This is how resigned fatigue becomes identity. It starts with legitimacy. A person hits a wall, then another. They scale down to survive. But instead of resting and rising, they remain. Struggle, no longer a passage, becomes a nameplate, and eventually, a barrier to reentry. Once people stop seeing motion as necessary, they stop recognizing stillness as a warning.

She didn't call it giving up. Most people don't. The language was softer. "I'm tired in a way that rest doesn't touch." "I've been through enough." "I just need to protect my peace." On paper, her life wasn't unstable. She had housing, some support from family, and no urgent emergencies. But participation had ceased. She kept the blinds closed. Meals were taken standing up. Conversations were rare and clipped. The days passed without confrontation or pursuit.

If enough people surrender quietly, the few who still strive begin to carry more than their share, until they burn out or walk away. And when they do, what remains is not chaos, but a smooth decay. A nation where nothing breaks visibly, but nothing is truly built. The body was still living, but the life had been set down.

This wasn't dramatic or visible. It was gradual. After a divorce and a long period of underemployment, she moved in with her brother "until she could figure things out." That was seven years ago. She had every intention of returning to something, work, school, independence. But the longer she stayed quiet, the harder it became to raise her voice. She turned down invitations. She avoided tasks that suggested responsibility. She carried herself gently, cautiously, as if life itself had become too loud. And those around her adjusted.

When expectation fades long enough, people begin to shrink to fit it. And the culture adapts to the new shape, designing systems that accommodate stasis instead of growth.

Psychologist Martin Seligman (1975) described this as a kind of learned futility. In his early experiments, animals were exposed to repeated shocks they couldn't escape. After a while, they stopped trying, even when the way out was clear. Their stillness wasn't fear; it was conclusion. They had learned that nothing they did made a difference. Years later, Seligman saw the same response in people. When effort changes nothing for long enough, the will to act begins to fade. What follows isn't fear. It's a quiet certainty that trying is useless. Years later, Seligman would revise and expand the theory to include explanatory style, how people interpret failure. Those who saw difficulty as personal and permanent were most likely to give in. And when that interpretation is reinforced, by others who stop expecting, by systems that stop pressing, it settles into identity.

Burnout isn't just a state of exhaustion any more. It's become a genre. Entire industries buy into it: articles, podcasts, retreats, endless digital confessionals. They all treat weariness as something to claim instead of as something to recover from. It offers legitimacy and softens judgment, but beneath that mercy lies the quiet risk of permanence. What once called for recovery now asks for reverence. Fatigue turns into identity. The burned-out self turns sacred, untouchable, unchallenged, endlessly protected from the very friction that might restore it.

This isn't to dismiss pain. Nor to deny real breakdown. But the shift is visible. We've moved from describing what we're going through to describing who we are. The difference is quiet but profound. "I'm overwhelmed" can pass. "I'm the kind of person who can't handle pressure" begins to reshape the future.

That reshaping doesn't happen in isolation. It spreads.

In families, burned-out adults start setting the tone for how much can be asked. In workplaces, they influence policies meant to protect, but often overcorrect. In schools, the language of fatigue is now fluent, even among the young. As psychologist Jennifer Breheny Wallace (2023) observes, "When children see the adults around them collapse under the weight of modern life, they assume that collapse is the normal response." Surrender becomes inherited. And effort starts to look like denial.

This is where the cultural shift takes root. When struggling becomes expected, and rising becomes exceptional. When exhaustion moves from symptom to self-description. When the very act of trying again feels naïve.

But trying isn't naiveté. It's muscle. It builds slowly. It doesn't need to be flashy or perfect or uninterrupted. It only needs to continue. And that continuation becomes harder to access when the cultural current is flowing in the opposite direction.

Lukianoff and Haidt (2018) cautioned us of this inversion in the way institutions now manage distress. They forewarned that modern safety culture encourages young people to treat discomfort as danger. Instead of learning to manage difficulty, students are increasingly taught to avoid it or hand it off to authority figures for resolution (p. 30). You've heard it in practice, "See something, say something." Though they were describing schools, the same reflex now shapes much of public life. Safety, once defined as the absence of threat, is now often defined as the absence of demand. And demand, even of the mildest kind, begins to feel oppressive.

When struggle is always interpreted as harm, growth becomes inaccessible.

The woman I once knew was not broken. She was careful. And small. Not in intellect or value, but in motion. She had once been bright, opinionated, engaged. Now she lived inside soft routines. No major crises, no risks, no reach. Her world had narrowed to what could be controlled completely, and what wouldn't ask too much of her.

That narrowing wasn't chosen in a moment. It was absorbed. By repetition. By reinforcement. By the slow quiet of people no longer expecting more. By institutions that asked less. By media that celebrated survival without asking where it was going.

When struggle stops moving, surrender begins to feel like peace.

But it isn't peace. It's suspension. It's a version of life designed for maintenance. And it is increasingly common.

Accommodation at Scale

It didn't begin with laziness. It began with overwhelm. With the well-meaning impulse to ease the load. Educators, clinicians, and service workers saw what people were carrying and asked less of them. But over time, easing the load turned into removing it altogether.

Accommodation, scaled wide enough, becomes culture.

In schools, it started with compassion. A child who struggled was given extra time. A teen who missed too many classes was offered leniency instead of consequence. The changes seemed humane. But each adjustment had a message beneath it: expectation hurts. Over the years, that message stuck.

By the 2010s, grading was often less about what was learned and more about what could be justified. Deadlines were moved for those who didn't ask. In many classrooms, boundaries shifted with emotion. What used to be clear became uncertain. Even the word rigor started to sound harsh, as if asking students to try harder might do some kind of damage. Teachers who kept their standards met pushback from students, parents, and administrators. To keep the peace, structure gave way.

The same pattern appeared in medicine. Patient satisfaction began to outweigh judgment. A person could describe fatigue or anxiety and leave with a diagnosis, sometimes even a prescription, without ever being asked a real question. The silences during counseling sessions, that once made room for thought, grew rare. Treatment drifted from guidance toward reassurance. As author and psychiatrist Anna Lembke (2021) notes, "We've grown uncomfortable with discomfort, so much so that we treat even ordinary distress as pathology" (p. 48). Medicine, meant to foster resilience, began to reward withdrawal.

The same patterns emerged in social services. What once aimed to transition people toward stability now softened around permanence. Income assistance required fewer job searches. Disability claims, once provisional, grew harder to revisit. Housing programs rarely tracked progress toward independence. The focus shifted to maintenance. To prevent crisis, agencies offered long-term support with no clear off-ramp.

No one designed these changes as failure. They were created from empathy. But empathy without boundaries becomes drift.

Dr. Erika Christakis (2016), writing on educational systems, described this phenomenon as "the institutionalization of infantilization." Adults, especially those in caregiving roles, began to interpret stress in children and adolescents as unmanageable. Instead of teaching coping, they removed the cause. The result, she warned, was a slow erosion of functional confidence. Students didn't just need help. They needed protection from expectation itself.

The ripple effects are visible.

A student who is never expected to meet a deadline becomes an employee who struggles to start. A patient who is always told "you've been through a lot" stops reaching for more. A housing client who receives support without structure stops believing independence is relevant.

Over time, the patterns become reflex. Systems designed to elevate begin to absorb. People are shielded, buffered, paused, but never pushed.

Caseworkers describe it quietly. The man who never showed up for job training, but still received his monthly stipend. The mother who skipped every parent-teacher conference, but whose child's records reflected "active involvement." The teen who stopped turning in homework, but graduated because challenging him "might cause harm."

One administrator I spoke with described the turning point this way: "We stopped asking who someone could become. We only asked how to keep them from falling apart."

That shift feels small. It isn't.

At scale, this accommodation becomes its own logic. Trying becomes optional. Follow-through becomes rare. And when a person does push, they're often met with confusion or caution. "Don't be so hard on yourself." "You're doing your best." "There's no rush."

Sometimes that's true. But sometimes it's a script. A way to justify stasis when motion is needed.

In her research on learned helplessness, Carol Dweck (1999) distinguished between two mindsets: fixed and growth. The fixed mindset interprets struggle as evidence of inadequacy. The growth mindset sees it as part of development. Institutions that accommodate without reinforcing growth begin to train the former. They teach people to stay still.

This is how surrender becomes systemic. It isn't announced. It doesn't come with flags or failures. It comes through policies that no longer lead anywhere. It arrives through support that keeps people passive. It settles into cultural memory. And eventually, it becomes expectation.

By the time anyone notices, the threshold has already dropped.

What once was minimum effort now looks aspirational. What once was resilience now feels unkind. The systems we built to lift people up are slowly teaching them to lie down.

This isn't cruelty. It's caution, misapplied. Institutions didn't forget how to push. They grew afraid of what might happen if they did. In doing so, they stopped asking whether anyone might still want to rise.

Hope as Effort

Hope is often miscast. It's imagined as a feeling, or a vision, or a sudden clarity that lifts the spirit. But for people raised in low-expectation environments, hope doesn't appear that way. It doesn't land. It's not something to wait for. It's something to do.

In cultures where drift becomes default, hope isn't found in emotion. It's found in repetition.

This form of hope is harder to sell. It doesn't shine. It doesn't post well. It doesn't offer immediate relief. But it moves. It clears a corner of the floor. It checks the mailbox again. It takes a walk without a podcast playing. It makes the call, even when the last five went unanswered.

This kind of hope doesn't ask how you feel about trying. It simply invites the next step.

Some mistake this for grit. And in part, it is. But grit has been overframed as personal virtue. Something tied to performance. Something you cultivate for your own advancement. What's needed now is different. It isn't about climbing. It's about stabilizing. Making a life that can carry others, not just promote the self.

In a culture that treats exhaustion as identity, and systems that protect people from challenge, choosing to engage again becomes a form of cultural repair.

But that repair is slow. And slow effort is often misunderstood. Especially when those around you are still resting in place.

The person who tries again is rarely praised. They are more often met with quiet suspicion. What are they trying to prove? Are they judging the rest of us? Why don't they take it easier?

That suspicion serves a function. It keeps drift protected. It shields passivity from contrast. As long as no one moves, no one has to ask why they've been still.

This is what makes cultural repair so difficult. It's not the effort itself. It's the emotional friction that follows. The silent backlash. The internal doubt. The lack of return.

Resilience in this context doesn't mean thriving. It means staying engaged even when no one notices.

It means trying again without energy. Without applause. Without external validation. And doing so not because it will fix everything, but because it holds something in place. It preserves a thread of connection between who someone was, and who they might still become.

Psychologist Angela Duckworth (2016) wrote that grit predicts success better than intelligence or talent. But she also noted that grit grows when people see purpose in their effort, when their actions serve something beyond themselves. In a culture of surrender, that purpose must often be self-authored. It won't be offered. It won't be echoed. It must be chosen anyway.

And that choice is quiet. Most days, it doesn't feel like hope. It feels like folding laundry when your chest is heavy. It feels like showing up for work when no one cares. It feels like reaching out to someone who may not reach back.

It feels like the opposite of what the culture now defines as healing. It feels like moving forward while still wounded.

But that's what repair often requires. It doesn't wait for resolution. It moves anyway.

Someone once described recovery to me this way: "I didn't realize I was getting better until I noticed I was still here." He'd been drifting for years, moving between jobs and couches, losing track of time. What changed wasn't medication or a sudden insight. One morning he started volunteering his time at a food pantry. Then he kept showing up. A few weeks later, someone asked if he could lead a shift. He told me he wasn't sure he was ready, but he didn't want to be just another guy who disappeared again.

That's how repair begins. Not with certainty, but with a flicker of dignity. A choice to stay in motion.

Hope, in this form, asks more than most people realize. It doesn't just resist despair. It resists resignation. And it resists the cultural script that says healing must feel good to count.

It's rarely dramatic. It doesn't announce its return. But it recalibrates reality. Slowly. Locally. In one home, one relationship, one workplace at a time.

This is the kind of hope that doesn't sell, but saves.

And we need more of it.

Because resignation spreads. But so does motion.

THE LIVES THAT DON'T BUILD ANYTHING

The Downward Drift

They didn't yell much in the Ortega house. No one expected much, either. Anger took effort, and effort was scarce. The fridge was stocked with drinks and processed food. The bathroom door didn't quite shut. The floor sagged in one spot near the hallway. No one fixed it. No one complained.

Rosa, the mother, worked overnights at a distribution center. She slept during the day, mostly. When she was awake, she stayed in her room, streaming shows or scrolling. She didn't cook. She microwaved. She didn't discipline. She threatened. The kids learned quickly that most of what she said didn't require a response.

Her oldest, Deon, was nineteen. Still at home. He'd enrolled in community college once but never went past the third week.

His room smelled like incense and energy drinks. He played music at night, but never too loud. He knew his mother wouldn't say anything unless the neighbors got involved.

His younger sister, Lani, was eleven. She made her own breakfast, packed her own lunch, walked to school alone. No one told her to. She just learned that asking meant waiting, and waiting meant nothing happened.

There were no family meetings. No check-ins. If someone cried, it was usually behind a closed door. If someone laughed, it was from something on a screen. They didn't eat together. Didn't plan holidays. Birthdays meant takeout and a cash app transfer. No one hugged unless someone else initiated. That didn't happen often.

Rosa didn't mean harm. She just didn't see involvement as part of the job. Her own mother had been worse, off and on drugs, with a rotating cast of boyfriends. Rosa learned early not to ask for help. When she got pregnant at sixteen, her mother kicked her out. She slept in a cousin's garage for two months. Since then, Rosa paid her own way. That was enough.

The message she passed down wasn't spoken. It was lived: take care of yourself, don't expect anyone to show up, and avoid trouble when you can.

Deon didn't rebel. He coasted. He kept his head down. Took a job at a vape store, quit after a week. Said the manager was rude. Said it wasn't worth minimum wage. Rosa didn't argue. She was too tired. She said, "Do what you want, just don't get locked up."

Lani started skipping homework in sixth grade. Her teachers sent emails. Rosa never answered. They left voicemails. She listened halfway, then deleted them. When the school called about Lani's behavior, disruptive, disrespectful, Rosa told them she was dealing with "a lot right now" and hung up.

There were no consequences at home. No rewards, either. Just space. Just time. Lani spent most of hers in her room, door closed, earbuds in. If something broke, it stayed broken. If she got sick, she slept it off. If she wanted attention, she misbehaved at school. It was the only place anyone noticed.

Apathy doesn't always look violent. Sometimes it just looks like distance. A gap that widens with each non-response. Each unasked question. Each ignored call from the school. Rosa wasn't cruel. She just didn't engage. Deon wasn't angry. He just stopped expecting. Lani didn't melt down. She tuned out.

What held the household together was mutual disengagement, calibrated in silence. No one demanded more from anyone else. No one gave more than necessary. Survival was individual. Pain was private. Needs were inconvenient.

And when that becomes the rhythm of a home, it replicates. Lani begins to mimic the tone of Rosa, short answers, eye rolls, dismissive laughter. She speaks to teachers like they're intruding. She treats questions as accusations. By twelve, she's fluent in avoidance. By thirteen, she'll be out the door most evenings. Deon will barely notice. Rosa won't ask. If she texts, it'll be "where u at" with no punctuation. If there's no reply, she won't follow up. She'll go back to her show.

In houses like this, no one names what's missing. Love isn't gone, it's just quiet, disorganized, misplaced. Care isn't absent, it's unexpressed, unstructured, unreciprocated. Responsibility isn't resisted, it was never introduced.

This isn't neglect in the traditional sense. The lights work. The rent's paid. There's Wi-Fi and cold drinks and rides when someone asks the right way. But there's no adult modeling. No emotional anchor. No one steady enough to absorb conflict or strong enough to guide correction. Everyone operates in parallel, sharing space but not direction.

When kids grow up here, they don't emerge broken. They emerge unformed. They know how to avoid conflict, how to minimize contact, how to coast through a room without being seen. What they don't learn is how to lead, how to hold weight, how to respond when someone else collapses.

The drift begins early. And it doesn't look like falling. It looks like floating. Until one day, someone needs direction, and no one remembers how to give it.

The Builders Who Leave

Elaine hadn't planned to raise anyone. She never had children of her own. At thirty-nine, she moved back to her hometown to help with her sister's medical recovery, three weeks, maybe four. That was the plan. Instead, she stayed for eight years. Her sister, Dana, didn't get worse, exactly. She just never resumed full capacity. The fatigue lingered. Then the depression. Then the part-time job she swore she would start again next month, next spring, next school year.

In the meantime, Dana's two daughters needed rides to school, help with homework, dinner on the table, someone to show up for the parent-teacher conference. Elaine stepped in. She didn't make a speech about it. She just did what needed doing. The girls responded. They started brushing their hair again. Grades stabilized. The yelling in the house quieted. Elaine covered groceries. Took the older one to a therapist. Sat on the floor and helped the younger one build a diorama for social studies, hand-cutting tiny pieces of paper to make the windows just right.

Dana thanked her sometimes. Usually after a wine buzz or during a holiday. "I don't know how I'd survive without you," she said one Thanksgiving. Elaine smiled. But by the following Tuesday, she was the enemy again for asking about job applications or reminding Dana about the unpaid utility bill.

Over time, the girls grew more attached to Elaine than to their own mother. They didn't say it, but everyone could feel it. Dana began pulling back, sleeping later, speaking less. Her irritation increased in proportion to her disengagement. The more Elaine took on, the more Dana seemed to resent her.

There were no fights. Just accumulating slights. Dana "forgot" to text her when school schedules changed. She stopped helping clean up dinner. She started claiming Elaine was "controlling" when she suggested budgeting. Eventually, she refused to ride in the same car if Elaine was driving.

Elaine held on longer than she should have. She believed her presence was stabilizing something fragile. And it was. But she underestimated what it was costing her.

She had stopped dating. Stopped traveling. Put off a promotion that would have required relocation. Her savings thinned. Her back hurt more days than not. She missed her old friends, but explaining why she hadn't left yet felt embarrassing. They didn't understand what it meant to be the only functioning adult in a house of near-adults and a sister who hovered just above collapse.

What broke her wasn't an explosion. It was Dana shrugging when the girls asked who was making dinner. "I guess if Elaine doesn't feel like helping tonight, we'll just have cereal." That was it. One sentence. Elaine finished the week, packed quietly, and left a short note. "I love you all, but this isn't love anymore. It's something else."

In the months that followed, Dana told friends and family that Elaine had abandoned them. The girls reached out a few times, but the messages grew infrequent. Without Elaine, the household lost its rhythm. Bills piled up again. One of the girls dropped out of school.

Elaine didn't come back.

She paid a high price for leaving. The grief didn't feel clean, it came laced with guilt, anger, loss. But she knew, in the marrow of her body, that she couldn't go back to being useful in a place where use was mistaken for obligation and care was mistaken for control.

We tell ourselves that builders are strong, and they are. But strength isn't limitless. It can harden into something brittle. Especially when unacknowledged. Especially when repaid with resentment.

The person who carries others rarely gets credit for the structure they maintain. They are background. Expected. They keep track of the calendar. Remember birthdays. Know which drawer the scissors are in. They mediate fights and schedule appointments and refill prescriptions. They buy the socks and set the alarm. Most of the time, no one notices, until they stop.

When they leave, the absence is felt, but not always understood. The collapse is framed as coincidence or sabotage. People ask: why now? Why like this? They forget to ask what it took to stay.

And that's what many builders carry, a quiet awareness that if they stop, something falls. Sometimes someone. It is a terrible kind of power. It doesn't feel empowering. It feels like being trapped in the knowledge that you matter more than anyone wants to admit.

Eventually, some choose themselves. Not out of selfishness. Out of self-preservation. The choice is rarely applauded. Often, it's punished. But in that choice lives a truth most people spend years avoiding: just because you can carry it doesn't mean you should.

Elaine doesn't tell the full story to people she dates now. She just says she had a long chapter of caretaking. It's true. And it's done.

The Stillness that Sinks Us

When a system fails, we expect a signal. Sirens, headlines, a public reckoning. Something unmistakable. What we rarely recognize is how often failure arrives with silence. No confrontation. No refusal. Just a steady draining of presence and function. Someone doesn't follow up. Someone else forgets the password. The trash stays full. The check doesn't get mailed.

Collapse hides in small forfeits.

This is what happened in the Baxter household. Not the dramatic kind, theirs was a home where things looked fine on the surface. Both parents worked. The kids were in school. There were groceries, working lights, even a new TV mounted above the fireplace. But no one was steering anymore.

The father, Greg, had checked out a year earlier. He still drove to work, but his attention was elsewhere. He didn't join dinner unless asked. Didn't remember which classes his son was taking or what day the mortgage was due. If the car needed repairs, it stayed broken for weeks. If someone in the house was upset, he assumed someone else would handle it.

His wife, Janine, used to hold the center. She organized the family calendar, cooked most meals, monitored grades, made dentist appointments. But after her mother's death and a bout of health issues, her capacity slipped. She stopped initiating. Requests now sounded like nagging. She didn't want to be a nag. So she stopped.

Their teenage daughter, Nicole, began spending more time at a friend's house across town. The son, Marcus, fifteen, started vaping. When his grades dropped, no one noticed until the report card arrived. Greg glanced at it, nodded once, and went back to his screen. Janine meant to talk to him about it but never found the right moment. She didn't want to fight. Didn't want to cry. Didn't want to hear him say, "So what do you want me to do about it?"

Everyone was waiting on everyone else to act.

This is what collapse often looks like, no villains, no breaking point. Just a family with no functional core. Not because they didn't care, but because care without leadership doesn't organize anything. It comforts, sometimes. But it doesn't move anything forward.

What fades first in these systems is coherence. Tasks get done sporadically, if at all. Birthdays are forgotten. Medical forms remain unsigned. The emotional climate becomes reactive, irritation instead of insight, withdrawal instead of correction. No one names the disrepair. Naming it would require action.

The children start modeling what they see. Not the values they were once told, but the behavior they live inside. They learn how to wait things out. How to keep requests vague so no one's responsible. How to interpret disengagement as normal, even inevitable.

When these children become adults, they don't collapse in dramatic ways. Most of them function. But function without direction breeds a kind of circular survival, always moving, never becoming. They pay bills late, but not disastrously. They have jobs, but not ambition. They parent, but without authority. They grow older, not upward.

In institutional terms, this is how cultural infrastructure thins. Leaders aren't replaced. Standards aren't renewed. Norms are passed down through tone instead of teaching. Schools adapt to parents who don't respond. Clinics adjust to families that miss follow-up care. Employers lower expectations not because they want to, but because the alternative is turnover.

It doesn't take widespread disaster to hollow out a culture. It only takes enough people waiting for someone else to act.

The tragedy isn't the absence of capacity. It's the abandonment of it. In houses like the Baxters', there are people who could lead. Who once did. Who still know how. But their energy has been spent on accommodation, on avoidance, on years of trying without return. So they stay quiet. They tell themselves it's not their turn anymore. Or not their place.

Meanwhile, the younger generation comes of age in houses where no one insists. No one follows through. They learn compliance by convenience. They offer emotional reactions in place of responsibility. They build lives with tools they've never seen used properly.

What gets passed on isn't brokenness. It's passivity. And it moves faster than anyone wants to believe.

HOW WE MIGHT BEGIN AGAIN

The Return of Grit, Grace, and Guardianship

Grit as Quiet Rebellion

There was a time when effort secured survival, but not admiration. In many places, it still does. In the coal towns of Appalachia, men descend into darkness each day to scrape a living from walls that barely hold. Their bodies wear out before their names are known beyond a county line. No viral clips, no admiration campaigns, only a steady offering of strength, absorbed and often unseen.

Grit, in these places, is not a narrative of personal triumph. It is rebellion against drift. To keep rising, when ease calls louder. To lift burdens, when the world whispers you deserve better. To work beyond what is visible, knowing the work itself may never validate you.

Endurance today is countercultural. In a world calibrated for immediacy, the decision to stay in difficulty looks almost reckless. Resilience has become a private rebellion, not a public virtue.

Real grit resists spectacle. It turns away from platforms that reward curated struggle. It refuses the performance of perseverance, the neat arc where hardship pays off in applause or influence. Grit as rebellion accepts that some loads are carried with no audience, and no payoff but the integrity of the act itself.

Across cultures, endurance once shaped identity more than expression. Among the Sámi reindeer herders of the far north, survival meant months of raw monotony: the scrape of metal against ice, the breath that froze in fur, the steady pulse of animals against a white horizon. They didn't talk about hardship. They worked through it, day after day, in a cold that didn't forgive mistakes. What mattered wasn't the story, it was what stayed standing after the storm.

In Japan before industrialization, a similar ethic shaped ordinary life. Gaman, to bear the almost unbearable with quiet patience, was expected within families as much as in the public square (Lebra, 1976). Children were taught not to collapse publicly under strain, because community stability required internal resilience.

These traditions were not romantic. They often demanded more than fairness would suggest. Yet they built a kind of human fortitude that could absorb failure without fracturing, disappointment without despair.

In contrast, much of modern discourse around resilience frames it as extraordinary, a rare trait, something to be developed through programs or interventions. But the truth is simpler and harder: resilience grows where endurance is lived without announcement. Where effort is its own proof.

False recoveries often mimic grit. They erupt in grand declarations of change, bursts of effort designed to be noticed. A worker burns bright for a season after years of drift. A student "turns it all around" with a burst of energy and collapses again the moment reward lags. Without quiet, repetitive labor, without loyalty to the unseen, the revival dissolves into another cycle of effort abandoned.

Sustained endurance rarely looks like momentum. It looks like monotony. Choosing repetition over retreat. Finishing when finishing feels meaningless. Showing up when the story no longer flatters.

Grit today is deeply unglamorous. It asks us to work toward futures we may not live to see. To plant seeds whose fruit others will eat. To withstand the loneliness of unseen work without twisting it into martyrdom or bitterness.

This is not just a personal call. Culturally, it matters whether we rebuild a tolerance for delayed outcome. A society that expects reward to immediately follow effort cannot build anything lasting. Communities grow brittle where effort is treated as exceptional, and endurance as tragic.

What endurance requires now is a different imagination. A vision that stretches beyond a single life. A willingness to live small, to work faithfully, to fail privately, and to try again anyway.

Grit as quiet rebellion will not trend. It will not offer emotional returns on demand. It will not soothe the modern craving for significance. But it will keep the fabric of culture from tearing further.

And it will give the next generation something firmer to stand on than sentiment.

Grace Without Rescue

Real grace does not dissolve consequences. It does not intervene to spare someone from the weight of their own choices. It allows difficulty to do its slow work without turning away from the person enduring it.

We have learned to confuse grace with relief. The instinct to rescue, to soften, to absorb the burden ourselves, often parades as compassion. But relational repair that rests on rescue is brittle. It demands that one person remain strong and the other stay small. No true restoration grows from that imbalance.

Grace, when stripped of its sentimental varnish, honors autonomy. It offers presence without domination. It recognizes that people must carry their own mistakes, and their own recoveries, if they are to own their futures.

In real relationships, grace often looks like restraint. It is the parent who stays close while a teenager faces academic consequences.

It is the friend who listens to the chaos of bad decisions without engineering a solution. It is the spouse who steps back when patterns must be broken from within, not imposed from without. Grace without rescue is active, but not invasive. It stands with, not over. It offers solidarity, not solutions.

This posture feels unnatural at first. In many family systems, love has been coded as intervention. To love was to spare. To care was to fix. We learned to measure connection by how quickly someone moved to relieve our discomfort. But that form of attachment teaches helplessness as much as affection.

In high-functioning cultures, repair is relational, not parental. Among the Akan people of West Africa, wrongdoing is addressed communally. The wrongdoer is called before elders and peers to face what was done and to begin to make it right (Gyekye, 1996). In that process, grace doesn't erase the damage; it grows from shared recognition and the slow work of repair that must be chosen, step by step.

In Jewish thought, the idea of teshuva, usually spoken of as "repentance", asks for more than apology. The one who has done harm must change course and seek forgiveness, yet forgiveness never cancels what's owed. Relationships mend not through words but through proof, shown in the steady pattern of changed behavior over time (Dorff, 1996).

Both traditions understand what many modern models lose: relational grace demands movement from both sides. The wounded must remain open. The wrongdoer must change course. Grace is not static. It breathes, stretches, expects.

When rescue substitutes for grace, the cycle calcifies. The person making mistakes feels no urgency to change. The person offering rescue becomes resentful or exhausted. What starts as love curdles into duty. What starts as generosity becomes obligation.

True relational repair often includes silence. Waiting for the other to choose differently. Allowing consequences to unfold without interference. Offering encouragement without manipulation.

It also demands humility. Grace acknowledges that not every breach will close. That some people will not return, or will return unchanged. To practice grace is to extend the possibility of repair without demanding the outcome.

The small generosities that strengthen relationships, the patient conversation, the willingness to forgive what has been owned, the steadiness in the face of slow change, are acts of courage, not comfort.

Grace without rescue holds the tension that modern life tries to dissolve: the tension between compassion and consequence, between presence and pressure.

There is a warning buried in this tension. Without it, relationships become extraction points rather than places of growth. One person carries the emotional labor for two. Repair becomes impossible, because real change is never required.

The easier path, rescue, over-functioning, solving on behalf of others, feels like movement, but hollows out connection. Grace requires the harder work of stepping back without stepping away.

In homes, this might mean letting a young adult face eviction after repeated irresponsibility, while still offering a door open if effort returns. In friendships, it might mean declining to enable a cycle of self-harmful behavior, while remaining available for a different conversation. In marriage, it might mean refusing to carry both sides of communication, trusting that change must be mutual or not at all.

Grace is not the abdication of love. It is love that refuses to substitute itself for the other person's agency.

And though it may seem colder at first, it builds the only kind of strength that lasts: strength owned, not borrowed.

Guardianship as Steadiness

The strongest systems are not built by those who flash brightest or move fastest. They are built by those who stay. Those whose presence endures after the excitement fades, after the applause dies, after the next emergency calls attention elsewhere.

Guardianship is not about crisis. It is about constancy.

To guard something, a family, a community, a standard, requires a long memory and a stubborn heart. It asks for patience that will be mistaken for passivity, commitment that will be mistaken for rigidity. It demands showing up, over and over, when nothing calls for it but the quiet knowledge that your presence matters.

In traditional societies, guardianship was not a specialization. Neither was it optional. It was simply understood. The elders stayed in the village because someone had to remember what held the place together. Memory and steadiness were a kind of shelter. Among the Navajo, the word hózhǫ́, often rendered as "walking in beauty" or living in harmony, carried a similar weight. Wisdom keepers were meant to hold balance across generations (Witherspoon, 1977).

In the small farming villages of Eastern Europe, age carried authority earned through work. Grandmothers and great-uncles ran the land, settled quarrels, passed down trades, and showed what endurance looked like in daily life. The presence of the older generation wasn't ornamental; it was the frame that kept everything standing.

In both contexts, what mattered wasn't visibility. It was rootedness.

Today, guardianship has been hollowed by mobility, by anonymity, by a cultural fixation on personal reinvention. Adults are urged to keep options open, to preserve flexibility, to avoid becoming "stuck." Stability has been quietly rebranded as stagnation. Presence has been treated as surrender.

The cost has been measured not in headlines but in the slow erosion of trust. Children grow up without anchors. Communities dissolve without custodians. Institutions lose memory because no one stays long enough to remember.

Guardianship resists this drift. It stays not because it cannot leave, but because it chooses to remain responsible.

This does not mean staying everywhere, in every relationship, under every condition. Guardianship does not require martyrdom. It does not mean tolerating dysfunction indefinitely. It means recognizing where your commitment builds more than it costs, and choosing to live there with deliberateness.

In practice, guardianship looks unremarkable. The teacher who stays in the same school district for decades, shaping not just students but the culture of learning itself. The small-town mechanic who trains an apprentice instead of competing with him. The foster parent who quietly becomes a child's only experience of consistency, without fanfare.

These acts rarely attract attention. They do not produce documentaries or viral posts. They produce something harder to quantify: a memory of steadiness in a world of fluctuation.

Steadiness does not mean rigidity. Guardians adjust. They respond to change. They bend without breaking. But they do not uproot themselves for novelty or abandon the work when recognition fades.

There is a risk in living this way. The work is often unseen. The returns are slow. Gratitude is rare. Those who commit to guardianship must develop an inner economy of meaning, where significance is measured not by reward but by faithfulness to what they chose to carry.

This mindset stands against much of what modern culture promotes. We are urged to optimize, to monetize, to scale our contributions. Staying local, staying small, staying faithful appears wasteful in a system built on movement and metrics.

But human thriving has always depended on those who didn't abandon their post, simply by refusing to walk away.

False models of guardianship can emerge when presence becomes performance. The leader who stays visible but withholds substance. The parent who remains physically present but emotionally absent. The community elder who clings to position but forgets the purpose behind it.

True guardianship is quiet. It requires continuous investment, not just continuous presence. It asks, again and again, not "how am I seen?" but "what am I sustaining?"

There is no guarantee that guardianship will reverse cultural drift. Some structures collapse despite steady hands. Some families fracture despite steadfast love. Guardianship does not control outcomes. It safeguards conditions where better outcomes remain possible.

In this sense, it is an act of hope. A decision to remain faithful to what is needed, not what is noticed.

The cost of abandoning this role grows over time. Without guardians, communities forget what they are defending. Without steady figures, children mistake movement for maturity. Without memory bearers, every crisis feels unprecedented, every solution improvised.

To be a guardian today is to work upstream against a current that prizes newness over endurance. It is to believe, stubbornly, that there are still things worth preserving even if no one thanks you for it.

And it is to trust that the seeds you plant in steadiness will outlast the noise.

CONCLUDING THOUGHTS
What Remains When We Stop Trying

Collapse does not always roar. It slips in quietly, when standards lower, when striving fades, when personal agency thins out under the slow comfort of neglect. What once demanded effort now only asks for feeling. What once built character now shields fragility.

Throughout these pages, we have traced the drift. A single branch of a family tree, once alive with movement, now sagging under its own resignation. Not broken yet, but heavy with the weight of what is no longer growing.

Some still build. Some still try. Yet the difference between the two has widened into a divide: those who expect life to demand something of them, and those who expect life to adjust around their refusals. The longer that split endures, the less visible the bridge back becomes.

We do not just inherit names or features. We inherit postures. Children watch how adults meet disappointment. They observe what happens when effort is honored, or excused away. They absorb whether striving is seen as natural or exceptional. That absorption, quiet and daily, becomes the baseline of their own adulthood.

Decline rarely arrives in grand moments. It arrives when difficulty is treated as harm. When low effort becomes self-protection. When ambition is framed as arrogance. These changes do not replace systems overnight. They replace expectations first, then habits, then identities.

We live now in a climate that normalizes withdrawal. A culture that rewards grievance over growth. Systems designed to elevate have softened into platforms for passive validation. Institutions once tasked with challenging the human spirit now retreat from the risk of expectation.

When effort disappears, so does meaning. When striving ends, so does stewardship. What remains is not peace. It is drift, families unanchored, relationships unmended, generations untaught.

This is what we pass down when we let go without knowing it: a model of disengagement disguised as self-care, a legacy of lowered thresholds mistaken for compassion. The quieter the abdication, the harder it is to name. The less we name it, the deeper it roots.

Children raised in such soil will not know what was lost unless someone shows them. They will assume passivity is natural, that discomfort is injury, that effort is suspect. They will build identities from avoidance and wonder later why nothing holds.

The inheritance of less is not carved into stone. It is whispered into daily habits. It is shaped by who still tries, even when trying costs more than quitting.

A Return Worth Making

If you are the one who still tries, who holds standards in a house that treats them as optional, you are not wasting your strength. You are the living proof that standards can survive discouragement. You are giving shape to the unseen ethic a child will one day call normal.

Children do not memorize lectures. They memorize patterns. A boundary held without apology. A job finished without drama. A promise kept without excuse. These are the silent tutors of character. These are the things that survive even when language fails.

Even in a house divided by effort, the one who keeps showing up leaves a mark. A quiet carrier, unnoticed in the moment, becomes the reference point later. The memory of a boundary held, a dinner made, a voice steady in conflict, these shape what survival alone cannot.

There are no guarantees. No action ensures a future reclaimed. But every standard maintained, every expectation honored, leaves behind something stronger than critique: it leaves evidence that life can be lived another way.

Legacy is built through daily friction. Through what we reinforce, what we tolerate, what we repeat without applause. One branch of the family may wither. Another may harden under the same conditions, not through chance, but through stewardship.

That stewardship demands repetition without immediate reward. It asks for faith in unseen seasons. It requires presence when no applause is offered and no outcome is guaranteed.

You may not see the fruit in your lifetime. You may only see resistance. But the standard you hold may be the one memory that sparks an awakening later, a quiet echo reminding someone that work is not shameful, that effort is not cruelty, that endurance is not weakness.

This is the slow repair. The return worth making.

Not a revolution. Not a call to grand action. A return to the foundation we abandoned when we mistook ease for care.

The branch does not have to break. It only needs to be strengthened, again and again, by someone who refuses to believe that drift is destiny.

That strengthening begins when someone stops adjusting to collapse and starts living by deeper measures.

Small standards. Quiet endurance. A posture of stewardship even when the world around you says it isn't necessary anymore.

When you refuse to excuse what weakens, you interrupt the inheritance of drift. When you keep showing up even when it costs you, you build more than a moment, you build a future someone else can stand on.

You become the branch that holds.

If this book stirred something in you,

... a sense that we've grown too comfortable with standing still, that effort and purpose still matter, you might find these titles worth exploring:

Ethical Hustle

A candid look at ambition, ethics, and the illusion of the "easy win." Learn what it means to build success without sacrificing integrity in a culture that rewards shortcuts.

Think Sharp

For those ready to move from observation to action. A practical guide to thinking clearly, deciding wisely, and reclaiming focus in a noisy world.

The Great Divide

A sharp, often wry exploration of how our national conversations fractured, and what it will take to argue, listen, and lead without losing our humanity.

References

Abidin, C. (2021). *TikTok and the "Platformed" Memes of Trauma*. Social Media + Society, 7(4). https://doi.org/10.1177/20563051211063855

Baumrind, D. (1966). *Effects of authoritative parental control on child behavior*. Child Development, 37(4), 887–907.

Beattie, M. (1987). *Codependent no more: How to stop controlling others and start caring for yourself*. Hazelden.

Bellah, R. N., Madsen, R., Sullivan, W. M., Swidler, A., & Tipton, S. M. (1985). *Habits of the heart: Individualism and commitment in American life*. University of California Press.

Berglas, S. (2014). *Stay hungry and kick burnout in the butt*. Harvard Business Review Press.

Bourdieu, P. (1986). *The Forms of Capital*. In J. Richardson (Ed.), *Handbook of Theory and Research for the Sociology of Education* (pp. 241–258). Greenwood.

Bowen, M. (1978). *Family therapy in clinical practice.* Jason Aronson.

Brown, B. (2012). *Daring Greatly: How the Courage to Be Vulnerable Transforms the Way We Live, Love, Parent, and Lead.* Gotham Books.

Brown, B. (2021). *Atlas of the heart: Mapping meaningful connection and the language of human experience.* Random House.

Cain, S. (2012). *Quiet: The Power of Introverts in a World That Can't Stop Talking.* Crown Publishing Group.

Christakis, E. (2016). *The importance of being little: What young children really need from grownups.* Viking.

Conrad, P., & Bergey, M. (2014). *The impending globalization of ADHD: Notes on the expansion and growth of a medicalized disorder.* Social Science & Medicine, 122, 31–43. https://doi.org/10.1016/j.socscimed.2014.10.019

Crittenden, P. M. (2008). *Raising parents: Attachment, parenting and child safety.* Routledge.

Darling, N., & Steinberg, L. (1993). *Parenting style as context: An integrative model.* Psychological Bulletin, 113(3), 487–496.

*Journal of Experimental Social Psychology, 48*https://doi.org/10.1016/j.jesp.2011.07.006

Davis, M. H., Ray, T., & O'Neil, M. (2012). Shared negative attitudes and group bonding: The social glue of complaint.

(1), 165–168., E. N. (1996). *The way into tikkun olam (repairing the world).* Jewish Lights Publishing.

Duckworth, A. (2016). *Grit: The power of passion and perseverance.* Scribner.

Duffy, B. E. (2017). (Not) *Getting Paid to Do What You Love: Gender, Social Media, and Aspirational Work*. Yale University Press.

Eberstadt, M. (2019). *Primal screams: How the sexual revolution created identity politics*. Templeton Press.

Ehrenreich, B. (2001). *Nickel and Dimed: On (Not) Getting By in America*. Metropolitan Books.

Ehrenreich, B. (2009). *Bright-Sided: How Positive Thinking Is Undermining America*. Metropolitan Books.

Feather, N. T. (1991). Attitudes toward the high achiever: The fall of the tall poppy. Australian Journal of Psychology, 43(3), 183–196.

Festinger, L. (1954). A theory of social comparison processes. Human Relations, 7(2), 117–140.

Fraser, N. (2013). *Fortunes of feminism: From state-managed capitalism to neoliberal crisis*. Verso Books.

Fry, R. (2020). *More young adults are living at home amid the coronavirus pandemic*. Pew Research Center. https://www.pewresearch.org/short-reads/2020/09/04/a-majority-of-young-adults-in-the-u-s-live-with-their-parents-for-the-first-time-since-the-great-depression/

Furedi, F. (2001). *Paranoid parenting: Why ignoring the experts may be best for your child*. Chicago Review Press.

Gheytanchi, A., & Joseph, D. (2020). *Parental burnout: An overlooked consequence of modern parenting*. Journal of Family Psychology, 34(5), 584–597.

Gibney, B. C. (2017). *A generation of sociopaths: How the baby boomers betrayed America*. Hachette Books.

Gopnik, A. (2009). *The philosophical baby: What children's minds tell us about truth, love, and the meaning of life*. Farrar, Straus and Giroux.

Greenfield, B., & Fisher, L. (2020). Accommodations and expectations: The ethics of psychiatric disability disclosure in the workplace. Journal of Medical Ethics, 46(6), 395–400. https://doi.org/10.1136/medethics-2019-105614

Grewal, Z. (2020). "*The Illusion of Influence: How Virality Redefines Success and Identity.*" Journal of Media Psychology, 32(3), 144–158. https://doi.org/10.1027/1864-1105/a000251

Gyekye, K. (1996). African cultural values: An introduction. Sankofa Publishing Company.

Haidt, J., & Lukianoff, G. (2018). *The Coddling of the American mind: How good intentions and bad ideas are setting up a generation for failure*. Penguin Press.

Hersey, T. (2022). *Rest is resistance: A manifesto*. Little, Brown Spark.

Hochschild, A. R. (1983). *The Managed Heart: Commercialization of Human Feeling*. University of California Press.

Hofstede, G. (2001). *Culture's consequences: Comparing values, behaviors, institutions, and organizations across nations* (2nd ed.). Sage Publications.

Horwitz, A. V. (2021). DSM: *A history of psychiatry's Bible*. Johns Hopkins University Press.

Illing, S. (2022, March 15). *Why everyone is quitting their jobs right now*. Vox. https://www.vox.com/the-highlight/22977663/great-resignation-workers-pandemic

Illouz, E. (2007). *Cold Intimacies: The Making of Emotional Capitalism*. Polity Press.

Lavrence, C., & Lozanski, K. (2014). "This Is Not Your Practice Life: Lululemon and the Neoliberal Politics of Spirituality." Canadian Review of Sociology/Revue canadienne de sociologie, 51(1), 63–84. https://doi.org/10.1111/cars.12033

Lebra, T. S. (1976). *Japanese patterns of behavior*. University of Hawaii Press.

Lembke, A. (2021). *Dopamine Nation: Finding balance in the age of indulgence*. Dutton.

Lukianoff, G., & Haidt, J. (2015). *The Coddling of the American mind*. The Atlantic. https://www.theatlantic.com/magazine/archive/2015/09/the-coddling-of-the-american-mind/399356/

Lukianoff, G., & Haidt, J. (2018). *The Coddling of the American Mind: How Good Intentions and Bad Ideas Are Setting Up a Generation for Failure*. Penguin Press.

Lythcott-Haims, J. (2015). *How to raise an adult: Break free of the overparenting trap and prepare your kid for success*. Henry Holt and Co.

Maier, S. F., & Seligman, M. E. P. (2016). *Learned helplessness at fifty: Insights from neuroscience*. Psychological Review, 123(4), 349–367.

Metge, J., & Kinloch, P. (1984). *Talking past each other: Problems of cross-cultural communication*. Victoria University Press.

Miller, A. (1981). *The drama of the gifted child: The search for the true self* (R. Ward, Trans.). Basic Books.

Murray, S. (2021). *The Therapeutic Turn: How Psychology Altered Western Culture*. Routledge.

Noddings, N. (2002). *Starting at home: Caring and social policy.* University of California Press.

Odgers, C. L., & Jensen, M. R. (2020). Annual Research Review: Adolescent mental health in the digital age: Facts, fears, and future directions. Journal of Child Psychology and Psychiatry, 61(3), 336–348. https://doi.org/10.1111/jcpp.13190

Parker, K., Graf, N., & Igielnik, R. (2019). *Young adults in U.S. increasingly unsure of adult status.* Pew Research Center. https://www.pewresearch.org/fact-tank/2019/10/23/most-young-adults-in-the-u-s-dont-think-they-have-reached-adulthood/

Peterson, J. B. (2018). *12 Rules for Life: An Antidote to Chaos*. Random House Canada.

Petersen, A. H. (2019, January 5). *How millennials became the burnout generation.* BuzzFeed News. https://www.buzzfeednews.com/article/annehelenpetersen/millennials-burnout-generation-debt-work

Plomin, R., & Daniels, D. (1987). *Why are children in the same family so different from one another?* Behavioral and Brain Sciences, 10(1), 1–16.

Putnam, R. D. (2015). *Our kids: The American dream in crisis.* Simon & Schuster.

Radesky, J. S., Schumacher, J., & Zuckerman, B. (2015). *Mobile and interactive media use by young children: The good, the bad, and the unknown.* Pediatrics, 135(1), 1–3. https://doi.org/10.1542/p eds.2014-2251

Reeves, R. (2022). *Of Boys and Men: Why the Modern Male Is Struggling, Why It Matters, and What to Do About It.* Brookings Institution Press.

Sapolsky, R. M. (2004). *Why zebras don't get ulcers.* Holt Paperbacks.

Schor, J. (1991). *The overworked American: The unexpected decline of leisure.* Basic Books.

Seligman, M. E. P. (1975). *Helplessness: On depression, development, and death.* W. H. Freeman.

Sennett, R. (1998). *The corrosion of character: The personal consequences of work in the new capitalism.* W. W. Norton & Company.

Siegel, D. J., & Bryson, T. P. (2012). *The whole-brain child: 12 revolutionary strategies to nurture your child's developing mind.* Bantam.

Siegel, D. J. (2015). *The Developing Mind: How Relationships and the Brain Interact to Shape Who We Are* (2nd ed.). The Guilford Press.

Stevens, A. (2017). *The psychology of disability: Hidden losses and unexpected gains.* Routledge.

Taylor, M., & Blum, A. (2023). *Patterns of emotional dependency and adult functioning in emerging adulthood.* Journal of Family Psychology, 37(2), 117–132. https://doi.org/10.1037/fam0001034

Truglio, R. T., Lovelace, V., & Fisch, S. M. (2000). *Evaluating the impact of media exposure on children's development: Scientific research and public policy.* Children and Media, 10(1), 43–56.

Tufekci, Z. (2015). *Algorithmic Harms Beyond Facebook and Google: Emergent Challenges of Computational Agency.* Colorado Technology Law Journal, 13(203), 203–218.Boyd, D. (2014). *It's Complicated: The Social Lives of Networked Teens.* Yale University Press.

Turkle, S. (2011). *Alone together: Why we expect more from technology and less from each other.* Basic Books.

Turkle, S. (2015). *Reclaiming conversation: The power of talk in a digital age.* Penguin Press.

Twenge, J. M. (2017). *iGen: Why today's super-connected kids are growing up less rebellious, more tolerant, less happy, and completely unprepared for adulthood.* Atria Books.

Ungar, M. (2013). *Resilience, trauma, context, and culture.* Trauma, Violence, & Abuse, 14(3), 255–266.

U.S. Census Bureau. (2021). *Historical marriage trends in America: Age at first marriage by sex, 1890–2020.* https://www.census.gov/data/tables/time-series/demo/families/marital.html

Van der Kolk, B. (2014). *The body keeps the score: Brain, mind, and body in the healing of trauma.* Viking.

Vance, J. D. (2016). *Hillbilly elegy: A memoir of a family and culture in crisis.* Harper.

Wildfire, J. (2023). *The performance of pain.* Aeon. https://aeon.co/essays/how-we-created-a-culture-of-passivity-and-performance

Witherspoon, G. (1977). *Language and art in the Navajo universe.* University of Michigan Press.

Yehuda, R., Halligan, S. L., & Grossman, R. (2001). *Childhood trauma and risk for PTSD: Relationship to intergenerational effects of trauma, parental PTSD, and cortisol excretion.* Development and Psychopathology, 13(3), 733–753.

www.ingramcontent.com/pod-product-compliance
Lightning Source LLC
Chambersburg PA
CBHW070628030426
42337CB00020B/3952